adopting darrell

A mother's faith journey

in parenting a profoundly

difficult child

Carol Weishampel

Carol V. Weishampel, Ed.D

HANNIBAL BOOKS
www.hannibalbooks.com

To order more copies of *Adopting Darrell*

Contact the publisher:
Hannibal Books
P.O. Box 461592
Garland, Texas 75046-1592

CALL: 1-800-747-0738
Fax: 1-888-252-3022

Email: hannibalbooks@earthlink.net
Visit: www.hannibalbooks.com

Order form on page 128 in back of this book.

Copyright Carol V. Weishampel, 2005
All Rights Reserved
Printed in the United States of America
by United Graphics, Inc., Mattoon, IL
Cover design by Greg Crull
Illustrations by Carol V. Weishampel
Unless otherwise noted, all Scripture quotations are taken from Holy Bible, New International Version, copyright 1973, 1978, 1984 by International Bible Society
Library of Congress Control Number: 2004117806
ISBN 0-929292-59-6

Dedicated to

Everyone who loves a child
with special needs

May God bless the parents—adopted and foster—
grandparents, and the extended families
of exceptional children.

May God grant a special blessing on teachers, therapists,
social workers, doctors, and friends
who choose to love and help a child become
everything God intended him or her to be.

A Special Dedication to

Darrell's siblings—Cheri, Colleen, Grace, Phillip, Christina,
JoAnna, Nick, Joe, Roy, Cora, and Chris—who loved and
helped care for their strange little brother

Darrell's adoptive grandmother, Verna Weishampel, who loved
him as one of her extended family, and to the memory of my
father, Arthur Weishampel

Darrell's foster parents, who courageously cared
for the medically frail, difficult infant

TABLE OF CONTENTS

Chapter 1—Packages of Promise — 7

Chapter 2—Precious Preemie — 13

Chapter 3—Problems — 20

Chapter 4—Professional Tightrope — 30

Chapter 5—Foster Parents — 34

Chapter 6—Progress — 42

Chapter 7—Preparation for Adoption — 53

Chapter 8—Promise of Wisdom — 59

Chapter 9—Seeking Professional Help — 71

Chapter 10—Thank God for His Helpers — 90

Chapter 11—Painful Decisions — 94

Chapter 12—God's Purpose — 118

ONE

Packages of Promise

" . . . children born not of natural descent, nor of human decision or a husband's will, but born of God" (John 1:13).

The mail carrier honked as he drove up our gravel drive. I was surprised when he handed me four thick, manila mailers. Each bore the Texas Department of Human Service's return address. Weeks earlier, I had requested a copy of my adopted son's Children's Protective Services file. I never expected to be overwhelmed by four volumes of material.

Awed by the stack of mailers, I retreated to our back porch, sat down on the swing, and tore the taped flap off the top envelope. Darrell, my adopted son, ambled over to the swing.

"Hi?" Darrell intoned a question.

"Hi, yourself, Darrell", I answered. "Want to swing?"

Laughing loudly, he climbed up next to me, turned around, and kicked his legs. With both hands he patted the mailers that lay on my lap. Suddenly he grabbed the mailer on top and began to swing his outstretched arms from side to side. In flashing arcs across his thick body he swung the mailer.

Afraid the contents would spill out, I caught Darrell in a bear hug to stop his gyrations. He patted the mailer against his head and covered his left eye. Although Darrell was legally blind, he had limited vision in his left eye. By covering or pushing against his eye, he simulated light flashes and created light and dark contrast.

Distracting him, I swapped several pieces of junk mail for the mailer. My heart ached. Darrell had just celebrated his eighth birthday.

Small for his age, my son was a handsome, blond child with clear, blue eyes that did not focus. Nystagmus, an eye condition, caused jerky eye movement. Darrell's ready smile exposed a toothless grin. As the result of bottle decay, his top four teeth years ago had to be pulled. To the causal observer Darrell appeared to be an average, though hyperactive, three- or four-year-old. But Darrell could not talk, was not potty-trained, and had frequent, violent temper tantrums.

Bored with the junk mail, Darrell slid off of the swing to wander aimlessly down the length of the enclosed porch. Choking emotions, I silently watched his awkward gait. One moment he seemed to be dancing—the next, prancing. With hands flapping like a bird trying to become airborne, his outstretched arms zipped around his body. Suddenly he flopped down, frog-legged, with knees outspread, his feet on either side of his bottom.

"Darrell, sit right," I admonished. "Feet in front."

He straightened one leg in front of himself, turned his back to me, and giggled. As if he were trying to smooth out wrinkles, he rubbed the floor with both hands. Our cocker spaniel, Ebony, tried to sneak past him. She trotted too close. Darrell was able to grab her. He rubbed both hands rapidly up and down her back and chuckled at the feel of her fur. Ebony stood quietly until he let her go. I smiled to myself. God had sent Darrell into my life to teach me compassion and patience.

Five years before, in 1986, when Darrell arrived on the scene, I was a divorced, single parent with two grown daughters and an adopted six-year-old son, Nick. As a single parent I had adopted Nick. His young mother, a friend of my oldest daughter, could not cope with his developmental delays and medical problems resulting from his premature birth. Through therapy and medical intervention, his physical and developmental problems had been overcome. Feeling successful as a parent, I envisioned that the Lord had prepared me to parent another special child.

I glanced up from scanning the thick package of papers. I recalled the overwhelming emotions I had felt when I read a newspaper article featuring a Houston adoption agency. Spaulding for Children placed only special-needs children. The article emphasized the large number of children waiting for adoptive homes. The agency provided free services to families who would open their hearts and homes to one of these difficult-to-place children. Most of the children the paper featured were older than three or were part of a sibling group that needed to be placed together. Infants available for adoption were of minority races or had physical or mental handicaps.

Phone calls, office visits, home studies, paper work, and social workers became a regular part of our lives. I was certain that I wanted to add another child to my family. Looking through a photo album of available children had been somewhat like shopping from a catalog. A description of the child's history and a description of the child's special needs followed each child's photo. My heart ached to take each child home. My brain tried to rationalize which child would best fit into our circumstances. Who would be a brother or sister for Nick? My prayers included the names of children. One just might become part of our family.

I attended adoption classes and scrubbed my house for a home study. Several months passed before my worker called to congratulate me. She had a three-year-old little boy for us. My prospective son was legally blind and developmentally delayed. I didn't care. With God's help, I could cope with it. I was excited and eager for her to mail a photo of him and a brief case history.

I recalled holding that first photo of Darrell. Tears had blinded me as I tried to focus on an angelic-looking, blond toddler. Tears splashed on the papers when I read that, at about five weeks of age, he had been physically abused. His mother had shaken him. The resulting brain injury caused cortical blindness and possible retardation. When he was released from the hospital, the baby had been placed in foster care. He had remained with the same foster family until the present. The case report stated that Darrell was healthy and active. He could walk, but because he was small, he usually was carried. His lack of vision made his gait awkward. Darrell attended a half-day, infant stimulation program for speech delay and to improve his coordination. He took prescription medications that controlled seizures.

    I was overjoyed! I had been expecting a child with problems. God was sending us a child that was young, mobile, and seemed to be near "normal" in development. The report indicated that he seemed to have some functional vision. I knew that physical development could be delayed by lack of vision. I was excited. A brother for Nick. A challenge for me.

    That night I had begun to struggle with doubt. Could I parent a blind person? Since I was six I have worn strong glasses. Now I depend on contact lenses and bifocals. Could glasses or surgery help this little boy? As an artist and teacher I never had taken my vision for granted. I felt lost without my contacts. My world was a haze. How well could Darrell function?

    For several years I had taught early-childhood, special-education classes. My students' handicaps had varied from cerebral palsy, Down syndrome, hearing losses, and speech delay to retardation. Could I learn Braille? Would he need a cane? A seeing-eye dog? Could I provide what this child would require? I prayed anxiously that the Lord would find the best home for this little boy and that I would understand if that home was not with me.

    My concerns for parenting were relieved somewhat when I viewed a videotape of Darrell. The videotape was taken in his foster home. Clearly he did have some functional vision. He reached for and grabbed up some noisy toys. He tracked a flashlight beam and tried to catch the light. He definitely could see the sunlight streaming through a patio door and lifted his face to the sun. When Darrell's foster mom picked him up and carried him away from the door, he squirmed to get down on the floor. Darrell quickly scooted sideways on his bottom—one leg out, bottom over, leg out, bottom over, like a sidewinder snake. Back he went to the glass door. He then stood up and banged his flat palms on the door as he demanded to go outside. The social worker opened the door, took his hand, and helped him negotiate the doorsill. Darrell shook his head from side to side and laughed. His face tilted toward the sun that turned his blond hair white. He pranced in place, then dance-walked aimlessly around the enclosed patio.

I recalled jabbering to myself with excitement. Darrell was developmentally delayed, but he seemed to have a great potential for growth. He would not be the companionable brother Nick had been wanting, but I knew that Nick's compassion for babies would help him to understand Darrell's limitations. I was more than ready to visit my prospective son.

Our adoption worker had arranged for Nick and me to visit Darrell's foster home. Knowing it would be a seven-hour drive, I left home by 5 a.m. The day was a beautiful, spring, Saturday morning. The stars still glittered in a gradually brightening sky. We were on our way.

Nick slept in the back seat as I drove and watched the sunrise, with golds and pinks reflecting from wispy clouds on the horizon. Beneath the ever-changing sky I was lost in thought and prayer.

Would I be the best parent for this little boy? Would another, two-parent family be able to provide more for him? What did my grown daughters really think about their mom's crazy ideas? How could I prepare myself to train a blind child? Could he attend public school? Would he be in special-education classes or in a school for the blind?

"Dear Lord," I prayed. "Give me wisdom. Let me understand Your will for this special child."

I then began to understand the term "pray without ceasing."

The miles slipped past with the rising sun. Nick and I stopped for a quick breakfast picnic of juice, donuts, and bananas. We both were eager to continue on. Nick had watched the videotape with me but had made no comments. Now he asked many questions that I could not answer. "How can he get up and down the stairs at home? Can he feed himself? Can he play ball with me?"

At a hamburger stand with a playground we stopped for a quick lunch and a stretch. Darrell's home was in a small, rural town nestled amid rolling pastures and old-growth pine forests. We had just enough time to register at a tiny motel on the edge of town before our 2 p.m. appointment at the county social-services office.

Nick and I entered the crowded waiting room. Bob, Darrell's local social worker, warmly greeted us. He introduced us to the entire staff. From his visits to the office everyone knew Darrell and obviously cared a great deal for him. My adoption worker arrived from Houston to join Bob, Nick, and me in a cramped office. We crowded around a rectangular table loaded with stacks of paperwork, toys, paper bags of clothing, a typewriter, a phone, and two thick notebooks. We squeezed two more chairs into the room for Darrell's early childhood-intervention teacher and his speech teacher. Opening the bulging notebooks, Bob opened the meeting by briefly reviewing Darrell's birth history.

The back door slammed. It jolted my attention back to the mailers filled with Darrell's life story. As I read the seemingly endless reams of data, in my mind I could see the events unfolding like the story that follows.

TWO

Precious Preemie

"The Spirit himself testifies with our spirit that we are God's children" (Rom. 8:16).

"Dr. Gibson. Dr. Gibson. Report to the neonatal nursery." The squawking speaker startled the young pediatrician. He had not expected a birth tonight and had anticipated going home after rounds. Dr. Gibson murmured that he should call his wife as soon as he had examined the newborn. His small practice held few surprises. His wife had become accustomed to his having regular hours now that his hectic internship was several years behind him.

As Dr. Gibson entered the delivery suite, the delivery-room nurse handed him a thick chart.

"Mrs. Smith delivered by emergency 'C' section," the nurse stated abruptly. "Her fever increased. Fluid leak. Premature rupture of the membranes. Fetal heartbeat normal. Dr. Stark delivered a five-pound, one-ounce boy of approximately 34 weeks gestation at 8:05 p.m. Apgar scores are 9. He is vigorous, and he's all yours, Dr. G."

The nurse led him into the nursery, where she gestured toward a tiny, pale newborn lying in a warmer and still covered with blood and vernix. The baby's cord had been clamped and faintly pulsed to a stop. Dr. Gibson verified her oral report with the chart and then studied the infant's breathing and color. The nurse took the baby's temperature and began to gently give him an admissions bath. As the young doctor examined the infant, he called out five-minute Apgar scores for the nurse to record. Another 9. Very good for a preemie. Dr. Gibson could make a positive report to the waiting family.

In the small, brightly-lit labor and delivery waiting room, three generations waited restlessly. A chubby, blond toddler climbed over the arms of a row of green, plastic chairs lining the far wall. Her grandmother glanced blankly in the child's direction. Ignoring the child's squealing and bouncing, the grandmother's attention turned toward Dr. Gibson as he entered.

Dwayne Smith, a thin, young man with his back to the door, leaned against a window frame as he nervously flicked a cigarette into an ashtray already overflowing with countless butts. His long, dark hair was greased back into a low ponytail held by a rubber band. He wore faded jeans, scuffed Western boots and a t-shirt blazoned with a motorcycle logo.

"Dwayne," Dr. Gibson addressed the teen-aged father with familiarity, "your wife and son are fine."

"Great, Doc," replied the boy as he extended his grimy hand. "He's too early, right? Ya sure he's gonna be okay?"

With words of reassurance Dr. Gibson explained the infant's condition as a preemie. He assured Dwayne that the baby would be under close observation for a couple of days. The doctor suggested to the grandmother that she and Dwayne's young daughter, Crystal, remain in the waiting room while Dwayne accompanied him to recovery. Dr. Gibson picked up Linda Smith's OB chart at the nurses' station and reviewed the report for Dwayne. No further complications had ensued. Linda was out of recovery and was resting in a small ward.

The visit with Linda was uneventful. The 17-year-old mother was groggy and relieved that the whole ordeal was over. She complained about her stomach hurting and asked for pain pills. With a nod of her head she accepted Dr. Gibson's assessment of her newborn son and seemed content that Dwayne would take Crystal and Grandmother home soon. Linda dozed off as the pediatrician and new father left the room.

Dr. Gibson accompanied the quiet, pensive young father to the waiting room. Crystal happily stuffed chips into her mouth. She left a trail of crumbs as she continued climbing on the chairs. With a soda can in one hand and a vending-machine sandwich in the other, Grandmother slouched on a plastic armchair. With a grunt she acknowledged their return. Her attention was tuned to a TV re-run.

The doctors' lounge clock caught Dr. Gibson's attention as he stretched and flexed his shoulders. After 10 p.m. Tired from reviewing his patients' charts, he pushed his wire-rimmed glasses up his nose, gathered scattered reports, scraped his chair back, and stood up with a sigh. Draining the last dregs of cold coffee, he hurried to return the charts to the pedi-nursing station. He checked his watch one more time. His wife would understand, he thought, as he turned to check on the preemie before he started home.

The night nurse barged out through the neonatal nursery door and collided with Dr. Gibson. "Dr. G., I was just on my way to page you. Glad you're still here. The preemie doesn't look so good."

Entering the nursery, Dr. Gibson detected a low, grunting sound from the direction of the infant's isolette. The newborn's color was poor. Although he was awake, his eyelids fluttering, his activity level had decreased. The baby's breathing was shallow and rapid. Nothing to be alarmed about, but precautions had to be taken. Dr. Gibson ordered a sepsis workup, complete blood work, and cultures. An IV line was to be started through the large vein above his forehead. Worried, Dr. Gibson ran his fingers through his thick, blond hair and started toward his office to update the infant's chart.

Dr. Gibson was surprised and relieved to find the newborn's extended family still in the waiting room. Vending-machine wrappers indicated that the little family had stayed for supper and TV. Crystal was asleep on one of the chairs. Her bottles and other baby paraphernalia were gathered up in anticipation of leaving.

The doctor expressed that he was glad to be able to explain in person the changes in the baby's condition. He stressed to Dwayne that the symptoms were common in a preemie and that he would call the family if the tests detected anything serious. With a promise to visit Linda in the morning, the doctor returned to the lounge to call his wife again and to take a quick nap while he awaited the test results.

What a tragic situation for this particular family, the doctor thought, as he relaxed on a lounge cot. Caring for a preemie would be difficult for most parents. This young couple was unstable and poverty-stricken. Linda and Dwayne had run off when Linda was only 15 and pregnant with Crystal. During his junior year Dwayne quit school to support them. The couple, though known as Mr. and Mrs. Smith, actually never had married, because Linda would have lost Medicaid and much-needed food stamps. Dwayne's menial jobs were sporadic.

When she began bringing Crystal into the well-baby clinic that Dr. Gibson sponsored, Linda still was overweight from her first pregnancy. She took Crystal there for her shots. The doctor's tired mind was a jumble of impressions. He recalled that although Linda had missed or rescheduled some of the clinic visits, she seemed to be a caring, if somewhat indifferent, mother. The grandmother (or was she a great-grandmother?) provided a room for Linda and Crystal—and for Dwayne when he was around. Grandmother usually drove Linda and her daughter to their appointments. She seemed to be the caretaker of the family.

* * * * *

The digital clock on the bedside table read 3:15 a.m. as Dr. Gibson reached for the ringing phone. The Smith baby had become lethargic. His color was poor; his heart rate was increasing. Earlier test results had been inconclusive but didn't indicate any medical problems. By the time the doctor raced to the hospital, the 32-hour-old infant's condition had improved. The baby's heart rate was normal, his breathing sounds were good, and his color better. But now he appeared jaundiced. Dr. Gibson gave orders for the baby to be watched closely but not to be fed. The doctor would nap in the lounge. Approximately two hours later the infant had a similar episode, but again, his condition improved by the time Dr. Gibson was awakened and summoned to the neonatal nursery. Chest x-rays were ordered and read immediately. They showed no evidence of pneumonia or a heart murmur. The doctor reviewed tests conducted earlier that evening. He compared those results to the newest ones. IV medication and fluids were adjusted. Oxygen therapy was to be continued while additional tests were conducted.

Baby Smith's chart lay open on Dr. Gibson's desk. The doctor was puzzled. After the two episodes and tests on the 29th, he had questioned whether the infant had a PDA opening in his heart that was spontaneously shutting, but x-rays had not shown a heart murmur. The 30th had been uneventful, with no abnormal symptoms. Now, this morning, the baby appeared to have a significant heart murmur. The doctor had transferred the infant to the neonatal intensive-care unit (NICU).

Dr. Gibson was content with his small-town practice, but he felt excited by the challenge of this preemie. Treating this infant would keep him from becoming complacent, he thought. PDA. He pondered PDA. Patent ductus arteriosus. Could this be the problem? Some preemies with RDS (respiratory distress syndrome) were known to have a delayed, spontaneous closure of the ductus in the heart as a result of poor oxygenation in the lungs.

His educated medical guess was to treat each problem without causing additional complications. He already had placed the Smith baby under bili-lights for jaundice treatment. What other treatment should he follow now?

Close observation, constant monitoring, repeated blood gasses tests, an IV, and oxygen-assisted life support continued for the next 24 hours. September the first. The new month seemed to instill new life into the Smith baby. After gradually being weaned off the oxygen and the IV, baby Smith—now named Darrell—started bottle feeding. Dr. Gibson, although still puzzled, felt relieved.

Charted medical notes included brief reports of Linda's infrequent visits to see her son. Linda had arrived at the nursery late on the 28th in a wheelchair that Dwayne pushed. She became so upset by the sight of the cranial IV, monitor wires, and the oxygen hood that she abruptly had spun the chair around and wheeled herself back to her room. The hospital recorded no visits on the 29th. On the 30th, Linda stood by the nursery window with Dwayne for a while. Both parents refused invitations to enter and to touch their son. A hospital social worker made notations of her visits with Linda to explain Darrell's prognosis, to offer support, and to encourage Linda to visit and bond with their son. The next day, after Linda and Dwayne were advised of their baby's continued problems, they refused to see him.

"I must encourage Linda to visit and feed her baby," Dr. Gibson muttered to himself as he pushed away from his chart-cluttered desk.

Entering Linda's room, he was surprised to discover that she was packing a small tote bag.

"Hello, Linda. Are you being discharged?"

"Yeah. The doctor said I'm healing faster than they expected. I'm so glad to get out of here and get home to

Crystal. Grandma says she's really been terrible. Missing me, ya know," she mumbled. Trying to hide her agitation, she continued stuffing her belongings into a brown tote bag.

"Linda, sit down," commanded Dr. Gibson. "Look, your hands are shaking. You seem upset."

"I'm so scared!" Linda wailed, as silent tears streaked her cheeks. "He's so tiny and so sick. I'm afraid to touch him. Feel my heart, Doctor. It's so fast and loud! Can't you hear it? Maybe he caught a bad heart from me!"

Trembling, she jumped up without waiting for an answer. She searched through drawers and stuffed additional items into her bag.

At last the doctor's gentle, sympathetic words calmed her. Linda agreed to go with Dr. Gibson to see Darrell before the hospital discharged her. She also vaguely promised that she would visit Darrell as often as Grandmother or Dwayne could bring her.

Linda kept her promise and visited to feed her son. Darrell slowly gained strength. He experienced no other episodes of distress. For the following two weeks test results were consistently normal. Darrell regained his birth weight. The hospital made preparations for his discharge. Meanwhile, Linda attended parenting classes at the hospital to help her learn to care for her preemie. In her reports the social worker noted that Linda seemed adequately prepared for the infant's transition home.

Dr. Gibson handed Linda an appointment card for Darrell's first well-baby clinic. He patted her shoulder encouragingly and then turned to write up his discharge summary. Linda beamed from the attention and well-wishes of the nursing staff as she left the hospital with her tiny, almost four-week-old infant.

THREE

Problems

"Be strong and courageous, do not fear or be dismayed . . ."
(2 Chron. 32:7a).

"Good afternoon. Children's Protective Services. May I help you? Yes, I am a social worker. My name is Teresa Harris, but you don't have to identify yourself. Yes, Dr. Gibson. You are required by law to report an injury to a child if that injury seems the least bit suspicious. Yes, I can take that information. I will tape-record this conversation and take notes.

"The child's name is Darrell Smith. How old is he? Five weeks? You say that this morning when his mother brought him into the clinic, he had a swollen, left forearm. X-rays show a break in both bones of the left forearm. What was the mother's explanation? Make sure I get this correct. The mother said that the baby had choked when she fed him, so she pulled him up by his arm to get him to catch his breath.

"That doesn't make a lot of sense to me, Doctor. You say that this is a feasible explanation? Hmm . . . .. Quickly raising the arms can help a baby catch his breath if he is choking? Alright. anything else? Yes, we do have information on the family. If this was an anonymous intake report, I couldn't tell you if we have had other reports, but under the circumstances, I can tell you that in addition to welfare and food stamps, we have provided some parenting intervention. I'm not allowed to give you any specific information, but I can tell you that we have not found evidence of suspected abuse of the other child.

"I will record your concerns, Dr. Gibson. Thank you for calling."

* * * * *

Teresa Harris, the social worker, made a routine newborn visit to the Smith home. She did not acknowledge prior knowledge of the baby's broken arm. Trying to be non-judgmental, she questioned Linda. When Mrs. Harris witnessed the baby gag on his formula, she accepted Linda's explanation of his choking problems. The social worker made some suggestions to ease Linda's problems feeding Darrell. As she rose to leave, she reminded Linda that she was always available to help.

* * * * *

Less than two weeks later, Mrs. Harris was surprised to receive a phone message from Dr. Gibson. The Smith baby was in the emergency room with his father and Linda's grandmother. The hospital was conducting tests. Dr. Gibson wanted to consult with Mrs. Harris as soon as she could reach the hospital.

She pulled off her glasses, tossed them on top of a pile of case folders, and then rubbed the bridge of her nose between her thumb and forefinger. Eyes squeezed shut, she could see the tiny, pale infant scrunched on his tummy into a corner of a full-sized crib. His mother stood over him and complained about his fussiness.

She prayed silently, "Dear God, did I miss something?"

* * * * *

Mrs. Harris glanced around the emergency-room waiting area and looked for the family of the infant. She was relieved that she did not recognize anyone as she hurried across the tiled floor toward the doctors' lounge. As she crossed a corridor, she glanced down the hall to her right. Dwayne Smith leaned against the wall outside of an examination room. His head hung down. His long hair hid his face. He did not see her.

Dr. Gibson answered Mrs. Harris' knock on the lounge door. Quick introductions were all that were required. Empathy joined their hearts. The young pediatrician was nervous, agitated, and pacing as he studied a series of x-rays that hung on viewers. Here, he pointed out, were the old fractures of the left arm. This other film revealed healing fractures of two ribs. The third film showed a fresh break in the right forearm. A final series of x-rays evidenced some swelling of the brain.

"If only I had ordered complete x-rays before," he admonished himself. "I'd have seen these old rib fractures and might have been able to prevent the new injuries."

The doctor did not hide from the social worker his astonishment. In residency or in his limited practice, he never had seen anything like this. Only in textbooks had he observed such a situation as confronted him. The x-ray showed a tense, bulging fontanel—swelling in the soft spot of the baby's cranium. Baby Smith was tachycradic and tachypnid—had a rapid heart rate and a rapid rate of breathing. These new symptoms were beyond comprehension of anything but abuse.

Dr. Gibson continued to pace as he addressed Mrs. Harris. "I thought I knew these people," he said. "I don't understand this. What could have happened since I saw him yesterday when I re-taped his splint?"

Mrs. Harris sighed as she sat down on a straight chair. She withdrew from her purse a small tape recorder, snapped it on, and opened a legal pad. "Tell me what you observed. I'll take notes."

Dr. Gibson began, "Dwayne Smith brought the six-week-old infant, Darrell, to the ER at 1 p.m. Linda Smith, the baby's mother, stayed home with their daughter. The baby, Darrell, was very listless and pale. His eyes were glazed. His head appeared slightly swollen. I noted slight bruising at the right corner of the mouth and on the bridge of the nose and also above the left eye on the forehead. These marks were not present yesterday when I re-taped his arm splint. I ordered a complete body x-ray, a spinal tap for meningitis, and blood work.

"I questioned Dwayne extensively. The father's story is that the baby seemed alright last night. Baby was sleeping at about 4 a.m. when Dwayne checked on him before he left for work. Dwayne stated that when he returned home at noon, he found his son lying listless, eyes open, but not seeming to be breathing. Linda didn't know what was wrong. She had given him a bottle around 6 a.m. He had spit up a lot. She tried to give him another bottle around 9:30 or 10 this morning, but he would not take it. He just fussed and cried, so she finally put him in the crib.

"Dwayne called Grandmother home from work when he got there at noon. Grandmother verified to me that the baby spit up a lot. He choked often during feeding. He has had colic, she said, and he did not sleep a lot. She says that he is fussy all the time.

"Be sure our notes state that this is the second time I have seen the baby in ER since his release after birth. On the last ER visit, when I called you before, I documented the spitting up and colic."

Mrs. Harris stared at her notes. On her last visit with this family, had she overlooked indications of abuse? Oh, what guilt she felt! The baby was so pathetically tiny, especially with that splint on his arm. The day of her visit he had been active. She did not see him spit up excessively. He had the high-pitched wail of a preemie, but Linda did not seem upset by his cry. She remembered that Linda had just jiggled his bed until he quieted and went to sleep.

What if this incident were critical? Could she have been negligent in her assessment of the situation? The state agency's policy was to provide whatever social services are necessary to keep a family together, if at all possible. Children were removed into protective custody only when absolutely necessary. What a fine line could exist between accidental injury and abuse!

Mrs. Harris mumbled to herself, "I'm trained to make gut decisions and live with the consequences." Then she admonished aloud, "You didn't hear that, Doctor."

Dr. Gibson confided to Mrs. Harris, "I am, too. Regardless of training, it's gut feelings and intuition that count. I have not yet told the family the extent of his injuries. I received consent for tests for meningitis, x-rays, and the usual when they first sought help. I want you there when I talk to them."

"How are you going to explain that you called me in?" queried Mrs. Harris.

"I'll tell them the truth—that by law CPS must be notified of unusual medical findings. I would like you to stand by and be supportive to the family. Please make mental notes of how these people react and what was their response. We are not accusing them of abuse. Not yet."

Mrs. Harris responded, "Yes, we must watch for signs of nervousness—any indication that an accidental injury that has not been acknowledged may have occurred, especially with a jealous toddler in the house. I can't comprehend this being deliberate abuse, but this baby definitely is in danger. I'll seek custody immediately after I talk to Dwayne. And to Linda.

"I'm going to notify NICU of the situation and order the pediatric unit secured," Dr. Gibson concluded.

When confronted with the medical information on the extent of his son's injuries. Dwayne became defensive and angry. "You people think that we hurt him? You think somebody in this family deliberately hurt my boy? You're crazy! really crazy!

"We all love that kid. Why would anyone want to hurt a little, bitsy baby?" he stammered.

Grandmother defended the young family and herself. "He's a difficult baby. He's hard to care for. He screams. He screams loud and shrieks. He throws up and won't sleep," she added defiantly.

"High-pitched, piercing cries, and spitting up are common with preemies. Linda knew to expect that," interjected Dr. Gibson.

"And he won't take his bottle," continued Grandmother, "and he spits up all over the place. He never sleeps but for a few minutes.

"He worries us a lot," she lamented, wringing her hands. "He don't sleep but minutes at a time. We never get to sleep at night!"

"She's right! But nobody would hurt him. We just don't know how to take care of him," added Dwayne forcefully.

Mrs. Harris tried to soothe him. "We understand that, Dwayne. But we need to find out about his injuries so you can take better care of him more easily."

"Well, I just don't know. I've told you all I can," the young man said icily. He crossed his arms defensively across his t-shirt.

Dr. Gibson glanced at Mrs. Harris as both became suspicious of Dwayne. Is he covering up? He showed little emotion toward his son. He was cold and calculated. Was he scared? Worried?

Dr. Gibson excused himself to attend to the baby's test results. Mrs. Harris explained that she would go to speak with Linda. Dwayne and Grandmother refused her invitation to accompany her. They preferred to let her confront Linda alone while they maintained their hospital vigil.

Dwayne interjected, "Yeah, you talk to her without me. But I'll be there soon. I want to hear what she has to say, too."

Then Dwayne abruptly changed his mind. He insisted that he and Grandmother would precede Mrs. Harris to their house. She could follow.

Before they left, Dr. Gibson returned from NICU to insist that the baby must be admitted to the hospital before anyone left. Grumbling, Dwayne went to admissions to sign papers. The older woman followed him.

Mrs. Harris and Dr. Gibson conferred quietly in the hallway. The baby's injuries and symptoms were so complicated that the doctor proposed transferring him to Texas Children's Hospital. Mrs. Harris determined that immediately after her visit to Linda, she would talk immediately with her supervisor. She slipped into the nurses' station to phone her office and alert the supervisor of the case.

* * * * *

Mrs. Harris drove rapidly across town to a small, frame house in much need of paint. She hoped to arrive before Dwayne did. As she pulled into the weed-filled yard, Dwayne arrived in his dented pickup truck. Car doors slammed. The three converged to walk in silence toward the sagging porch. Through the open door, Mrs. Harris could see Linda watching TV as she reclined on a lumpy, over-stuffed sofa. A soda can and full astray sat on the floor beside her. Crystal played with a few broken toys scattered on the threadbare carpet. Laundry littered the spare furniture and spilled over onto the floor.

"How's my baby?" Without getting up she greeted Dwayne. Then her eyes fell on Mrs. Harris. "What's she doing here?"

"He's not too good," Dwayne answered glumly. "Not good at all."

Linda glared at him, then shifted her eyes to Mrs. Harris, who had followed through the door. "I said, 'What's she doin' here?'"

"Hello, Linda. I know you weren't expecting to see me again so soon. I'm Teresa Harris."

"I know who you are. You were here before. What are you doin' here now?" demanded Linda, as she sat upright.

"Because of the extent of your baby's injuries, the law required Dr. Gibson to inform CPS and to make a report," Mrs. Harris responded bluntly.

"Injuries! What injuries? My baby don't have no injuries! He's just sick!" Linda yelled, as she pushed herself up from the sofa to face the social worker.

"Now, Linda, I understand your being upset. I'm here to try to help you and your family take care of your baby," soothed Mrs. Harris. "I just need to ask you some questions."

"Yeah, well," responded Linda, calming down. "We do need some help. He's . . . He is a really hard baby to cope with. Them classes don't tell me about the screaming and throwing up and not sleeping."

"We understand that he has had a lot of difficulties, Linda. He is going to be alright," answered Mrs. Harris.

"Is that true, Dwayne? Is he okay?" Linda asked. "If he's OK, then where is he? Where is my baby?"

"Yeah, sure he's okay," Dwayne replied. "But Dr. G. said that he will have to stay in the hospital for observation. Isn't that right?"

Dwayne glanced at Grandmother, who had entered from the porch. She shrugged and sank deep into an armchair.

"What's wrong with him?" Linda questioned.

Dwayne answered solemnly, "They're saying that his other arm has been broken and two ribs are cracked. Something might be wrong with his brain."

"His brain!" Linda cried. "What do you mean that something's wrong with his brain? You just said he was OK!"

"It's nothing serious. I really don't understand, but Dr. G. said that the baby had some swelling in his head. They are going to do some tests and watch him. He said that the baby might have meningitis. Is that what he said?" Dwayne indicated to Mrs. Harris to back him up. "Meningitis?"

"Yes, I believe he mentioned meningitis."

"Well, what's that?" asked Linda. "Never heard of it."

"It's an infection that causes the brain to swell. That is why more tests are needed," replied Mrs. Harris.

"I guess they can go on and do the tests, but I still don't see why you're here." Linda confronted the social worker again.

"Linda. Dwayne. I'm here because we want to help you and your child. In order to do that we may need to take custody of him, so that he can get the best treatment possible," she answered gently.

"What do you mean? Take custody of my son?" demanded Dwayne.

"You have Medicaid for him but no insurance. From what I understand, the tests and hospital stay could be extensive and very expensive," she stated. Her statement implied that Medicaid might not pay for all of it.

"If CPS had custody, that does not mean that you are no longer his parents. This means that the state will take care of him and his medical expenses for you. We can help you. We can help you to get counseling and parenting training so you can take care of him."

"What if we don't want your help? We will just pay when we can!" Dwayne shouted defiantly.

"CPS will take that into consideration. Of course our first concern is for the care of your baby. I know that's your concern, too," Mrs. Harris appealed. "Your cooperation is very important for his recovery."

Mrs. Harris urged Linda to describe the events that led up to Darrell's latest hospitalization. Her story, although vague, was consistent with her husband's and her grandmother's reports. She did not admit to causing or seeing anyone else, including Crystal, cause the baby's injuries. She denied the injuries existed.

"You just go on now," Dwayne instructed, showing a nervous Mrs. Harris to the door. "We'll talk this over. And we'll let ya know what we decide—what we're going to do."

* * * * *

The judge was appalled by the case Mrs. Harris presented to him over the phone. He granted her an emergency hearing as soon as she could type up and present her case. Before the judge sat down for dinner, he had met with the social worker and her supervisor, reviewed the case, and awarded emergency, temporary custody of Darrell Smith to the Children's Protective Services. Immediate suspension of parental rights was granted.

The following morning, as soon as court convened, the court order was signed and recorded. Mrs. Harris, relieved by the legal action, rushed a copy to the hospital. Goals for the child included temporary foster care. Supervised parental visitation was to be encouraged pending investigation. Baby Darrell was now cleared to be transported, within the next few days, to Texas Children's Hospital for extensive evaluation.

FOUR

Professional Tightrope

"Commit everything you do to the Lord. Trust Him to help you do it and He will" (Ps. 37:5).

Dr. Gibson took Darrell Smith's medical file and entered into it the court order. The doctor was relieved about the transfer to Texas Children's. His notes for September 20th recorded that the infant had a seizure associated with apnea, an absence of respiration. He observed stiffening of the extremities. The baby's eyes deviated to the right. His skin was flushed. Darrell was loaded with Phenobarbital, a drug to combat seizure activity. A repeat lumbar puncture revealed bloody spinal fluid.

For September 21 Dr. Gibson noted that CAT scan results of the baby's brain showed acute blood in the ventricles and subarichnoid spaces, low density areas in the left frontal and right occipital lobes (probably secondary to edema of the area), and curvilinear low density in the left frontal region (probably secondary to a subviral or edema in the cortex).

Translated for Mrs. Harris, this report presented evidence compatible with the trauma of child abuse—probably the result of being shaken. The tiny infant's brain had been bruised inside of his skull. This caused some bleeding and fluid leak. Arrangements were made for Darrell's immediate transfer to Texas Children's Hospital for treatment of acute subdural hematoma (bleeding inside the skull).

The young doctor was troubled. Should he have been able to foresee these injuries? He was frustrated and apprehensive about the complications that indicated child abuse. Was he in some way responsible? Could he be held legally responsible for medical neglect? He no longer felt young—only inexperienced.

* * * * *

Teresa Harris sipped her tepid coffee, put the half-full cup down, and closed her eyes. Knowing Darrell was getting the best possible medical care compensated for the stress she felt in dealing with his parents. Her desk was littered with pages of the baby's extensive case file. Dr. Gibson's latest report prominently added to the top of the stack. He had scheduled the baby to be transferred by ambulance. The transfer would occur early the following morning. Mrs. Harris' job now was to inform the parents of the transfer. She also had located foster parents who would be willing to care for Darrell after his discharge.

Mrs. Harris determined to tackle locating foster parents first. Searching her files, she had to locate only three area families that might be willing to foster another child. Foster families were scarce. Each already had a maximum of six kids. She'd have to apply for a variance in order for a family to take an additional child. Her first and second calls produced negative results. Neither family would consider adding a critically ill infant to their already-large families.

The social worker's third call was to Marge and Joe. Earlier in the week one of their foster children had been returned to his parents. Yes, they would willingly add Darrell to their family of foster and adopted kids. The baby would help heal the ache of losing Peter. Teresa briefed Marge on the case. She stressed the infant's medical condition. Plans were made for Darrell's assessment at Texas Children's. Later Marge would accompany Mrs. Harris to the hospital to see Darrell and to develop a plan of service.

* * * * *

As she hung up the phone, Mrs. Harris put down another cup of forgotten, cold coffee. Darrell's birth parents had been agitated and angry during their phone conversations. Both parents had received court orders to be polygraphed. They were furious. Although Mrs. Harris tried to maintain her role as family advocate, the parents said the CPS worker was responsible for all their troubles. Her job was to grit her teeth, ignore their animosity, and inform them of the baby's impending transfer to Texas Children's Hospital.

At times like this the stress was so great that Mrs. Harris wanted out. Her gut told her that Darrell's parents were somehow responsible for abusing him. Or, at least, they knew something they were hiding. He was not safe with them. Her conscience and training insisted that parents were innocent without proof. Their rights must be maintained unless law terminated these rights.

She walked a thin professional tightrope. Her head ached. Mrs. Harris stared at a snapshot of Darrell. Both arms were in casts, his head was swollen, his eyes were sunken and dark. Wires from electrodes on his head connected him to machines. Her head dropped on her arms. She wept silently. And prayed.

Taking a deep breath and forcing composure, Mrs. Harris phoned again. As diplomatically as possible, she requested that Linda and Dwayne, as parents, accompany her when Darrell was transferred and admitted to the children's hospital.

Linda's response had been typical. "You took our baby. Now you take care of him!" she railed.

Mrs. Harris maintained her neutral role and waited. Finally, Linda stopped ranting. She agreed that early the next morning, Mrs. Harris could pick her up for the long drive. Dwayne had a temporary job. Understandably, he refused to go.

Mrs. Harris and sullen Linda arrived late—only moments before the ambulance transporting Darrell was to depart from the small, county hospital. The women followed as the ambulance sped out of town. The long road trip was tense with strained silence.

Linda did not acknowledge her sick baby as workers transferred his isolette from the ambulance through the hospital's emergency entrance and into an examination room. The two women signed admissions papers at the desk before hospital employees ushered the women into the exam room. A pediatric neurologist ignored their entrance until he had concluded his examination. He then addressed Linda concerning the baby's history. Linda answered his questions as though Darrell never had been separated from her. When asked whether Darrell smiled at faces and followed brightly colored objects, Linda said, "Yes." She said he could lift his head and could roll from his stomach to his back.

The doctor gave Mrs. Harris a quizzical glance. With a slight shake of her head Mrs. Harris met his eyes. The doctor made notes of their conversation as he observed the listless infant lying prone in the isolette. His notes described a lethargic baby that had poor head control–an inactive infant that was unresponsive to persons or objects. At two months of age Darrell functioned like a newborn.

The doctor excused Mrs. Harris and Linda as a team of specialists appeared in the doorway to complete Darrell's intake exam. Left to pace the hall, Linda insisted that Mrs. Harris take her home immediately.

FIVE

Foster Parents

"... you welcomed me as if I were an angel from God ..." (Gal. 4:14).

When Marge and Joe agreed to be foster parents for the sick baby, they knew they could rely on many years of experience fostering kids for CPS. By phone Mrs. Harris briefed them on Darrell's history and medical problems. She promised to mail them copies of his records. Marge was eager to be involved with the baby while he was still in the hospital. This would help her and Joe prepare to care for Darrell when the hospital discharged the baby. Because Joe, being retired, was capable of caring for their other kids, Marge was confident that she could make the trip to see Darrell while he was still hospitalized.

Mrs. Harris, who phoned the hospital, gave Marge and Joe daily updates. Darrell underwent extensive testing. A CAT scan confirmed subdural hemotomas with some split cranial sutures. Marge understood this to mean that Darrell had bleeding or fluid that caused swelling in his brain. His head now had swollen about one inch from the time he was admitted. Neurosurgery specialists had been consulted. The possibility existed that the baby would need surgery to implant a shunt to drain the fluid and relieve the pressure.

Sight unseen, Marge had taken this baby into her heart. She prayed for him and anxiously waited for each daily phone call.

Good news! The neurosurgery team did some subdural taps to drain the fluid. If the swelling did not return, Darrell would not require additional surgery. The baby finally was gaining a little weight.

The baby began having seizures. He was placed on Phenobarbital. Marge ached to hold and comfort "her" baby. She was eager to see him but was becoming even more anxious about her ability to care for him.

* * * * *

"What an exhausting day this has been!" sighed Marge as she leaned back against the headrest and closed her eyes while Mrs. Harris negotiated the traffic. Images of the tiny, pale infant with IV lines, bandaged arms, and a swollen head swirled in her memory. She had been overwhelmed and stunned by her first glimpse of Darrell lying so still and surrounded by medical paraphernalia. Recovering her composure by the strength of her compassion for children, Marge had insisted on being allowed to hold him. A lump had welled up in her throat again. She fought back tears. How could a human being, so helpless, endure so much? She wanted to hate the person who was responsible for his condition. Instead she prayed for the family. She prayed for Darrell.

Relaxing a little, Marge smiled to herself and recalled how the entire hospital staff assigned to "her" baby had convened in the nursery so that she could continue holding him, bundled in blankets and bandages with wires sprouting, while they conferred. Marge had felt as though she were some important personage on a dais. As she sat in a rocking chair, the staff focused its attention on her and Darrell. The staff presented medical facts, answered her questions, and accepted her as a team-player.

Everyone knew that Marge was accepting a tremendous responsibility. They must make sure that she was well-prepared for Darrell's home care. They briefed her on such matters as the signs of seizures, on medications, on the procedures for subdural taps, on the IVs, etc. Doctors reassured the women that the baby would not be discharged until he was stable and doing well.

Marge mentally located baby equipment and planned for the day that Darrell would come home. She agonized that the hospital staff could not rock and stroke and sing to him. She knew how busy they were. She also knew the tremendous healing power of love. She and her husband of 42 years relied on the Lord's love to draw their strength as parents, adoptive parents, and foster parents.

* * * * *

Less than a week later Marge again went to the hospital with Mrs. Harris. Darrell finally had stabilized. No seizure activity or swelling had occurred since the neuro taps. Today Marge could take him home.

Baby Darrell was free of IV's and looked less pale. Marge gently dressed him in a warm sleeper and wrapped him in blankets. The head nurse presented her with his seizure medication. She carefully reviewed detailed, written instructions for his care. Marge was encouraged to learn that the baby's parents could not contact her. They could see him only on weekly visits, to be scheduled at Mrs. Harris's office.

* * * * *

Marge and Joe were exhausted and discouraged. For the past two weeks they had shared the responsibilities for taking care of Darrell, taking care of their other children, and running their home. Neither Marge nor Joe had been able to sleep well. They had encouraged Darrell to take a bottle every two or three hours. Often he dozed off or refused to suck. They said he spit up. A lot.

If he fell asleep while Marge or Joe held him, he promptly woke up when they laid him down. His cry was high-pitched, piercing, and very annoying. Although he was lethargic for his age, when he was fully awake, he squirmed, grunted, and fussed. He often continued this fitful behavior when he seemed to be asleep. The elderly couple took turns trying to sleep, but neither could ignore his restlessness. They feared complications. They doubted their good intentions, but they would not admit defeat.

A visit to Dr. Gibson frightened Marge. Darrell's head had begun to swell again. He had not gained any weight since he had been with her. She had not noticed seizure activity, but she once had seen his eyes deviate to the right and upward. Such heavy responsibility!

Blood was drawn for a Phenobarbital level. Immediate arrangements were made for his re-admission to Texas Children's. Marge's stomach churned. She admonished herself. What should she had done differently? How could she have prevented this episode?

As they went over the pedi-neurologist's instructions, Joe calmed her and reminded her that they had done everything as they had been instructed.

An ambulance transferred Baby Darrell for the same neurosurgeon who had treated him before to admit him to the hospital. A neurology workup was done to determine if he needed shunt surgery. Again he had an inch of swelling of his brain. His weight was still nine-and-a-half pounds. He was extremely small, thin, and pale for three-and-a-half months of age. Marge fretted but was relieved that Darrell's care had been taken from her. She was determined to get some rest, get caught up on household chores, and to spend some quality time with her other children while Darrell was hospitalized. She rationalized her feelings of relief and guilt by remembering that she would be better prepared to care for him when he was discharged.

Marge and Joe anxiously waited for Mrs. Harris' daily phone reports. The day after admission, Darrell had a subdural tap. The next day doctors performed another tap without complication. Three days later while the tap procedure was in progress, Darrell began having seizures. His IV was loaded with Phenobarbital. He was put on oxygen. Because the seizure activity continued, he also was given Dilantin. The little guy toughed it out. Pacing the floor, Marge prayed for her baby. Wherever she worked around the house, Marge trailed the phone by its cord as she awaited a call from Mrs. Harris. A CAT scan now showed diffused blood in the baby's brain. How she longed to travel to the hospital to hold him, but the long trip and daily care for the other children kept her from going.

For the next few days Darrell's seizures occurred hourly; then they began to taper off. Finally the seizures were brought under control. His medication was adjusted to stabilize him. Marge's anxiety was relieved for a few days. Then, on Saturday, she received a call. Darrell had developed a low temperature. He had been placed in Pedi-ICU. Early Sunday morning, not being able to reach Teresa, Marge and Joe found a sitter for their other children and rushed to Darrell's cribside. The 12-hour round-trip exhausted them both mentally and physically. Through the thick glass they observed the baby while they held hands and prayed. Tears ran shamelessly down their cheeks.

Early Monday morning Marge made an unannounced visit to Mrs. Harris' office. On Sunday Marge and Joe had been very upset about Darrell's condition. The IV's in his head were bleeding. He was having hourly seizures again. He had lost all body temperature before he was placed under heat lamps. Besides, he had developed diarrhea and had to be taken off formula.

Marge shared with Mrs. Harris how they had stayed by Darrell's side, although outside the glass, during the crisis.

They refused to leave for home until after he had become stable. A call to the hospital assured the women that his temperature now was normal and his seizures were neither frequent nor as severe. He was not yet back on formula but was expected to return to bottle feeding the next day.

In her case notes Mrs. Harris wrote that Marge reported that she could not get Darrell to make eye contact when she had very briefly been allowed to hold him before they left. Marge had notified the on-duty doctor, who referred to Darrell's chart. He predicted that the extent of the brain damage was greater than the initial prognosis. Mrs. Harris wondered whether the foster parents would refuse to take the baby now. They were in their 60's but were very dedicated. Could they be expected to have the energy and the stamina to ensure his specialized care?

The next week Darrell experienced a week free from reaccumulation of fluid in his brain and only slight seizure activity. Discharge plans were being considered without surgery. Results of Darrell's neuro examinations revealed conditions essentially unchanged from admissions. He still was lethargic, with little spontaneous movement of his extremities. He was unresponsive to brightly colored objects, persons, or the environment.

Marge was overjoyed when Mrs. Harris called to make arrangements to bring Darrell home from the hospital. The baby's pediatrician was ecstatic that Darrell had improved so quickly after the trauma a week ago. The women rushed to reclaim the baby that tugged at their hearts. Both women eagerly made notes as the pediatrician and nurses reviewed written orders the hospital sent to Dr. Gibson as home-care instructions. Darrell still was experiencing slight seizures on the right side; therefore, he would continue taking Depekene and Phenobarbital. He had been placed on an iron-fortified formula. Although he still was having some diarrhea, he was keeping most of the formula down.

The pale, thin baby—his translucent skin ghost-like—was carefully and snugly bundled for his trip home. The women who loved him commented that they could see the acute, suture lines of his skull. They noticed that the area where the fluid had been drained was sunken.

The elderly mother and the social worker glanced at each other when Darrell began to cry—a weak, muffled tone like that of a starving kitten.

During the long ride home, Mrs. Harris updated Marge on the baby's legal status. The state's child-abuse team had reviewed the medical evidence and determined that his injuries probably were sustained on a minimum of two occasions. Possibly three separate incidents existed. The pedi-neurologist and other medical specialists had provided notarized affidavits for Dr. Gibson and to CPS regarding this final assessment of child abuse. Marge cried silently as she gently stroked Darrell's thin, blond hair. How could anyone possibly harm a tiny baby? She cringed, even more brokenhearted, because Mrs. Harris could not answer her question, "What will happen to him now?"

On the drive home, Darrell threw up his formula. He also had very bad-smelling diarrhea. The women agreed that Darrell should see Dr. Gibson the first thing the next morning. Tiny, weak, four-month-old Darrell was home for his first Christmas.

* * * * *

Christmas at Marge and Joe's home always was a close, extended-family event. Married children arrived with their kids. Grown foster kids dropped in to join the current kids in celebrating, playing, and eating. Love and family support permeated the home. Darrell was adored. Eager hands fed, changed, and rocked him. This eased Marge's tasks. A stronger, healthier baby greeted the New Year.

A few days later, Mrs. Harris took Marge and Darrell back to Texas Children's for follow-up exams by the pedi-neurologist. His reflexes and movement, at four-and-a-half months of age, were at the developmental level of a two-month-old.

Because of the recent trauma and the developmental delay that can go with prematurity, the extent of his brain injury could not be determined. His doctors predicted that they would expect to see more problems as Darrell grew older. They speculated that the extent of permanent brain damage soon would reveal itself. The affected parts of Darrell's body would be obvious. The baby still was taking only a few ounces of formula at a time, so his formula was changed. More calories were added to insure maximum brain growth.

The doctor then stated the women's unspoken fears. Because Darrell did not focus on near bright objects, the possibility existed that he was blind. His pupils dilated and constricted normally. This meant that his eyes were receiving visual messages, but his brain was not processing these images properly. The doctors could not determine just what the baby could see, so they should treat him as though he could see normally. They should use brightly colored objects to stimulate what little vision he might have.

Returning home Mrs. Harris assured Marge that the state would provide her with materials and therapists to help her stimulate all of Darrell's development.

During the next week Darrell continued to improve and grow stronger. He began to take more formula; the diarrhea finally decreased. Determining the extent of his brain injuries had been secondary to his survival, but now Dr. Gibson, too, had to verify that Darrell seemed to suffer from cortical blindness. He also determined that Darrell was having cerebral palsy-like symptoms in his head muscles. His seizures appeared to be under medical control. Although the baby continued to be irritable and fussy and his sleep was erratic, Darrell was a little easier to care for. As he approached five months, he was a little less fragile.

SIX

Progress

"It is more blessed to give than to receive" (Acts 20:35).

Marge worried as she rocked the fretful baby. Since Darrell had become stronger, she had faithfully carried him to the CPS office, where he had weekly visits with his entire birth family. Usually Dwayne, Linda, Crystal, and Grandmother showed up. The visits always were hectic. Everyone passed the baby around and played with him until he grew tired and irritable. She had to sit back and watch these people act as though they were a typical, normal family. Her stress level elevated. They ignored her until Darrell got fussy. Then Marge seemed to get the blame. They indicated she was spoiling him, not feeding him right, or dressing him too warmly. The family member who was holding him would hand him back to Mrs. Harris and ignore both Marge and Darrell while they tried to impress Mrs. Harris. Crystal destroyed the room.

For several days after each visitation Darrell would cry and fuss. His crying was different—more of a moan. He wouldn't eat and was fretful. Dr. Gibson could find no organic cause for his behavior. Could it correlate in some way to the family visits? Was he stressed? Marge kept copious notes on "her" baby.

As Darrell grew, he catnapped during the day but would not sleep at night. He preferred to play or cry. Marge and Joe took turns rocking and trying to feed him all night, every night. If

Darrell dozed off and they tried to put him down, he woke up and squalled. The devoted couple became physically and emotionally exhausted.

Darrell coughed up blood and was admitted into the county hospital with pneumonia. At five-and-a-half months of age, his weight only was 12 pounds. As he improved, he began an infant-stimulation physical-therapy program. A home therapist trained Marge to massage and flex Darrell's limbs. The therapist instructed Marge to use noisemakers, toys, and flashing lights to stimulate verbal response. A therapist scheduled home visits once a week to evaluate Darrell's progress and to update his stimulation program.

Marge and Joe worked out a mercilessly tiring routine. Joe shared housework, chores, and laundry duty while the other children were in school. The couple alternated napping during the day and rocking Darrell at night. Marge and Joe had to encourage him to take a bottle every three hours, but he never acted hungry. After school the older kids played on the floor with him. They tried out games that the physical therapist suggested. They amused him with musical toys and provided constant attention. Friends, neighbors, and extended family dropped by to help.

The family did not hold back love for the cranky, difficult baby. He thrived, although his development was delayed. At 10 months he weighed only18 pounds. His skin remained translucent and pale, but he was not as frail and delicate as he looked. He now could sit with support.

Darrell loved to be bathed! He sat, supported, in the kitchen sink and splashed water all over the counter and floor. Then he squalled when time arrived to get dry. Frequent ear infections made the pleasure of bath time stressful. He refused to tolerate cotton in his ears, so the fun of splashing had to be tempered with the fear of getting water in his ears.

Darrell's moods and temperament improved somewhat. He now babbled and laughed when he played with someone. For unknown reasons he continued to have many daily episodes of inconsolable fretting and squalling. His moods could change in an instant. No one understood what suddenly frustrated him into a screaming tantrum.

* * * * *

The time arrived for a follow-up visit to Texas Children's Hospital. The doctors were impressed with Darrell's weight gain and general improvement. Marge beamed as she related all of his minor accomplishments. Although severely delayed in motor and cognitive development, he was physically stronger and healthier. After an extensive examination, the neurologist repeated his diagnosis that Darrell was blind. In her heart Marge had known this prognosis but could not face it until she actually heard the doctor's words. She was devastated.

* * * * *

Mrs. Harris informed Marge that the courts had held a termination hearing to determine if enough investigative evidence existed to sever Darrell's parents' rights. The court found that Darrell suffered "optic atrophy and cerebral palsy secondary to hydrocephalus due to multiple blunt head traumas as part of the child-abuse syndrome."
Interpreted to Marge, this meant that Darrell either had been hit, or more likely, had been shaken so violently that his brain was bruised. This had caused it to swell and bleed. Marge shuddered as she repeated the information to Joe. The report verified their worse imaginings. Charges had not been filed on either parent. The case was still under investigation. Months would go by before the parental-rights case went to court.
A family party and cake for Darrell celebrated his first birthday. His "family" included Mrs. Harris, Dr. Gibson, therapists, CPS staff, and neighbors, as well as Marge and Joe's

large, extended family. Darrell batted brightly colored balloons and played on a crawl monitor provided by the Commission for the Blind. Darrell's favorite toys created a lot of noise. How he loved sounds! Rattles, bells, toys that made a variety of sounds, and especially the telephone fascinated him. The bright light of his new flashlight held his attention. He grabbed the flashlight and held it up to his left eye as he stared into the intense light. Marge and Joe were emphatic that he could see something.

Family members compared his birthday photos with pictures taken six months previously. They commented about his growth and personality changes. The loving, but tired, couple was beginning to feel successful as Darrell's parents.

* * * * *

Marge waited with an impatient Darrell, now 14 months old, for Mrs. Harris to take them for an eye exam by a pediatric ophthalmologist. Bottles, diapers, cookies, and toys helped console Darrell, who did not like being confined to a car seat. Fortunately for the women, he dozed for part of the long trip.

A comprehensive eye examination done while Darrell was sedated confirmed blindness due to optic-nerve deterioration and cortical injury. Much to Marge's dismay, no lens or surgery to improve the little boy's vision was available. Marge was heartened to learn that Darrell seemed to be able to see some light-and-dark differences with his left eye. At least his world was not completely dark. The doctor stated that he saw no way to confirm exactly what functional visual input Darrell's brain processed.

On the return trip Darrell, still sedated from the exam, slept peacefully. The women pondered his fate. In her own way, each prayed silently that more functional vision would become apparent. Mrs. Harris assured Marge that state agencies would be contacted to provide information and help so Marge could train him at home. The State Commission for the Blind would evaluate Darrell. It would determine what services the agency could provide for him.

*****

Darrell's second Christmas was an exciting challenge for his extended family. Each member tried to entertain and please him. He laughed and bounced to music but ignored the rest of the holiday festivities. Surprisingly he turned away from the cute, fuzzy stuffed animals that everyone "just knew" he would love to feel. Christmas photos were witness to his progress. He now could stand alone in his crib or playpen. He was hopping, not crawling, around on the floor. Darrell accomplished this by sitting frog-legged, knees out, with his feet beside his bottom. He then bounced on his bottom in the general direction of voices, the TV, or other sounds. He vocalized many sounds and could be very demanding. He no longer was passive and listless.

Shortly after the New Year, Darrell was taken for evaluation at the Retina Research Center. The Commission for the Blind had referred him. Marge and Teresa both had been praying that surgery would be available to improve his vision. They were taken into a room and asked to sit with Darrell at a table with a device that held two circles. One side of each circle was gray. The other side had gray stripes of varying sizes. The circle device was flashed approximately 100 times while a worker hit the table and jingled a bell. No one explained the purpose of the tests or how the results were obtained. No doctor examined the baby. The experience was inappropriate, pointless, and a waste of time.

Mrs. Harris confided to Marge that the test seemed to be strictly for research. Disappointed, they agreed that they would not give up their search for help.

*****

The courts began taking depositions for a hearing of criminal charges against Darrell's parents. The legalities of the case frightened Marge. She had not experienced this aspect of foster parenting. The complications and delays of the case wore on her nerves. Weekly parental visits had continued for the past year, except when Darrell was sick. Marge was sensitive to the birth parents' feelings and rights, but she still felt edgy when they tried to find fault with her in defense of their own lack of parenting skills. She dreaded the visits. Linda and Dwayne acted cocky and complained that they had been framed. Mrs. Harris no longer was their scapegoat. Marge had possession of their son, so she was guilty of causing all of their trouble. At these visits they spent little time getting to know Darrell.

* * * * *

Seventeen-month-old Darrell made his first airplane trip. Arrangements were made for him to be evaluated at the medical school in Galveston. Airport activity, voices, and people moving entertained him with new sounds. He was not fretful as long as his stroller was moving, or he was being carried. Fortunately for Marge, he took a bottle on take-off and slept during the flight.

A rented car transported Mrs. Harris, Marge, and Darrell to a motel, where they shared a double room. Although fussy at times, Darrell was unusually cooperative when he was fed and changed. How he loved being the center of attention! For the first time, Mrs. Harris participated in his routine care. She bathed him and laughed as he splashed water and soaked the rug and her blouse. She played with him and then fed him a bottle. Marge smiled and watched Mrs. Harris roll Darrell around on the floor. They both smiled as they listened to him giggle when he grabbed and shook toys that made noises. Instead of crawling, he still hopped around on his knees and his bottom. He discovered the phone cord hanging from the night table. He

47

grabbed the phone's curly cord and shook it so rapidly that the receiver flew off the cradle.

During the night Darrell woke up four or five times. He cried until Marge gave him a bottle or changed him. She sat on the edge of the bed and rocked and stroked his back as he drifted back to sleep. Marge was accustomed to the interrupted sleep and did not feel unusually tired the next morning. Mrs. Harris, however, woke each time Darrell did and felt the effects of interrupted sleep. She now could appreciate Marge's dedication, for Marge had not had an uninterrupted night's sleep in a year and a half. Even when Darrell was hospitalized, she automatically woke up during the night.

As the women dressed, Marge fed Darrell crackers. She was apprehensive about his behavior in the motel's dining room. He astonished her. He was intrigued by the medley of the sounds and smells and behaved while they ate breakfast. Smiling and babbling, Darrell acted almost like a normal toddler.

The women had difficulty locating the intake clinic at the medical school. They had to pass through several waiting areas. Marge cringed to see so many severely retarded and extremely handicapped children. The many poor children who were inappropriately dressed for the cold weather grieved her heart. Most did not have on shoes or coats. Although many young interns and medical students were around, they were in too much of a hurry to help with directions. They discovered that a third waiting area included an information desk for several different clinics. Many specialty services seemed to operate out of this branch of the medical school.

At last a social worker called everyone into a large conference room. Ten to 12 specialists introduced themselves. Pediatric specialists, various therapists (visual, speech, occupational, and physical), nursing specialists, social workers, and a few interns that drifted in and out surrounded the long table. All of these experts were to evaluate Darrell for their residency program. Each specialist pulled a pen from the pocket of his or her white lab coat, shuffled a legal pad, and took voluminous notes while they questioned Marge and Mrs. Harris and observed Darrell.

The experts keenly noted how Darrell responded to Marge while he was on her lap, how he responded to voices and laughter, and what movements he made when he was placed on the table or floor. Fortunately all of the attention kept him in a good mood. Rarely did anyone outside his home see his tantrums.

The first question asked Marge was, "Why have you traveled so far?"

Marge hugged the toddler and replied, "To get him all the help we can."

The committee asked about the services Darrell was receiving, the amounts of time spent daily in each of the therapy disciplines, what referrals had been made, and the results of specific examination. They wanted to know Dr. Gibson's prognosis. Each of the women was asked her concerns.

Every possible question was asked about Darrell's birth history, medical history, and development. Marge wondered if any of these people had read his case file. The file must have been studied, because without actually conferring, the team agreed that Darrell seemed to be a happy, healthy boy. They could not understand why CPS would consider removing him from his stable foster home to place him in a residential treatment facility. The hospital program had nothing to offer. Since he would get more attention in a home environment, they could not appropriately recommend moving him to an institution.

Marge shuddered. An institution? She had so hoped for more help for Darrell, but she had not considered the possibility of an institution. She was vastly relieved that no one had suggested this placement. He would not be leaving her.

On the flight home, Marge relived the realization that she could have lost Darrell if the doctors had a better treatment plan available. If left to her, if an option had existed, she cringed, could she make the decision to place him in a residency?

Darrell discovered that if he put his ear against the plane's window, he could hear the sound of the droning engines. He patted the window, put his ear to it, giggled, listened, and repeated the cycle over and over. He was actively listening more and was trying to repeat sounds. Sitting astride Marge's lap and facing her, he put his hand under her chin or across her mouth as she made silly sounds. He giggled and tried to make those sounds. He could be encouraged to say "ma, ma, ma, da, da, da" and "bye, bye."

* * * * *

Joe comforted Marge and tried to calm her. In tears she had returned from Darrell's weekly family visit. Linda had been changing Darrell's diaper. She rarely did this on the visits. Angrily she accused Marge of bruising him. Shocked with disbelief, Marge fled the room and left Darrell with Mrs. Harris and the birth parents.

Mrs. Harris confronted Linda. She insisted that Linda show her where she had seen bruises. Mrs. Harris insisted that Linda undress Darrell again. A secretary was called in as a witness. No bruising was found. Mrs. Harris ended the visitation and sent Darrell's parents home.

Mrs. Harris located Marge, wiping tears from her eyes, in the restroom. Mrs. Harris calmed the foster mom's fears. She reported that she had confronted Linda about the accusations. No bruising had been found. The social worker reminded Marge that she, herself, had changed Darrell and had helped bathe him during their recent trip. She speculated that pressure from the child-abuse charges, the investigation, and the definite possibility of permanently losing her son had caused Linda to lash out. Some people, she told Marge, try to make others look bad to make themselves look better. Marge understood that philosophy. Kids did this all the time. Marge was too emotionally involved with Darrell to think logically.

Marge confided to Joe that she was frightened. Linda would continue to look for bruising. Now that Darrell was standing and was more mobile, he fell often. Bouncing on his bottom he moved rapidly around the room. His pale-bluish skin on his thin body did bruise easily. The worried foster parents decided that they must document his falls.

* * * * *

Dr. Gibson had been treating Darrell for congestion and ear infections for most of his young life. Because he was concerned that Darrell may have a hearing loss, he referred him to an ear specialist. Fortunately, no hearing loss was found, but Darrell had to be admitted to the hospital to have tubes put in his ears to relieve fluid buildup and to have his adenoids removed.

The surgery went well, except that Darrell had a reaction to the anesthesia and turned red. Marge was elated that no major problems had occurred. For the next several weeks, she could not take him outdoors unless absolutely necessary. To prevent Darrell from getting a cold or infection, Marge could not allow him to be around other people. Hopefully the tubes would drain fluid from his ears; he could hear better and would begin to talk.

Dr. Gibson was consulted for a follow-up. Darrell remained on ear medication and antibiotics because he now ran a fever and pulled on his ears. Since the surgery Darrell had not been sleeping. Marge and Joe were exhausted. They wondered when their life would be less hectic.

Marge was pleased with the surgeon's follow-up exam. The infections had cleared up; the tubes were working as expected. Marge related to the doctor how Darrell pulled on his ears. To her surprise the doctor said that Darrell's ears were his sight. This was especially true now that he could hear better. Especially with all of the attention being paid to his ears since the surgery, Darrell was more inclined to feel them than was a sighted child.

* * * * *

The next several months were relatively peaceful for the foster family. A weekly routine with therapists' visits, structured playtime, and family activities emerged with Darrell an active member. Ear problems resolved, he was healthy but still had erratic sleep patterns. Nightly Marge slept in a rocking chair with him on her lap. Several times during the night he woke for a bottle or a diaper change. If she tried to place the sleeping toddler in his crib, Darrell woke with a start and cried. The rocking-chair routine allowed her to rest better. During the day Darrell took little of the baby food, finger foods, and bottles that she offered him. He just never seemed hungry.

SEVEN

Preparation for Adoption

"and we know that in all things God works for the good of those who love him . . ." (Rom. 8:28).

Summer passed quietly. The older children helped watch and entertain Darrell, who approached his third birthday. With his ears stuffed with cotton (which he finally had learned to tolerate), he loved to splash in the small wading pool or the bathtub. Fishing was a pleasure Marge had not been able to enjoy since she became Darrell's mom. Now she, Joe, and the kids worked out a system in which they could fish from a pier at the lake. Meanwhile, Darrell was safe in a playpen under the trees. When his wail let them know that he no longer would tolerate the confinement, Marge balanced him on one hip while she cast and reeled in with one hand, with her fishing rod tucked under her arm. Joe always was close enough to take the little boy or her rod if Marge got a nibble.

Parental visitations continued. Darrell was responsive to being the center of attention and allowed himself to be passed around from lap to lap. When he tired, he squirmed around to get down on the floor, where he could be more active crawling under the table, chairs, and grown-up legs. Linda usually held him for a while and gave him appropriate, motherly attention. Then, as he became more wiggly, she would begin to talk to other family member or to the staff. She would ignore him until he was put on the floor. She rarely discussed Darrell's progress but talked about herself and the upcoming legal hearings. Both criminal and civil child-abuse cases now were pending against both parents.

* * * * *

Darrell experienced a setback. For several weeks a physical therapist had been working on his motor skills. She encouraged him to walk while he held her hands. During this process he fell and hit his head. Now he refused to be coaxed into trying to take steps. Although she knew how erratic Darrell's movements could be, Marge blamed the therapist for the accident. Marge so much wanted for him to be able to walk, but now he was afraid to try. At her insistence a special helmet with a face guard was ordered for his protection.

Darrell's speech was not developing. A speech pathologist as well as a speech therapist saw him. He seemed to listen intently and, at times, would stop mid-play, become very still, cock his head, and listen carefully. He turned his head to locate or follow sounds. His many therapists reminded Marge and Joe that this indicated that he was becoming more aware of his surroundings and of the world that existed beyond himself.

Darrell's protective helmet arrived. It was to be used when Darrell attempted to walk or when he was on the ground in unfamiliar territory. He hated it. He screamed to let everyone know how much he hated it. He refused to cooperate with that thing on his head. Even with openings for his ears, it blocked some of his hearing. Now that he was more aware of sounds, any obstruction to sound frustrated him.

To locate himself in space he began to swing his outstretched arms, front and back, around his thin body. His bottom-bouncing locomotion developed into a curious sideways movement. Sitting frog-legged, he reached out to the side with one leg, then shifted his bottom in that direction. If he felt an obstacle, he stopped and reached over to feel it. If he reached a step-down, he checked the drop with his leg and kept moving down. If he reached something he could climb, he crawled up like a monkey. In the large, open, family room he traveled sideways quite fast. The family laughed as he slithered like a sidewinder snake or a fast inchworm inching along.

* * * * *

Mr. Davis, the CPS supervisor for the region, arrived to introduce himself to the foster family. He and Mrs. Harris cautiously approached the purpose of their visit. If Darrell's parents' rights were terminated when the child-abuse cases went to court, CPS was considering the possibilities of placing Darrell for adoption. Marge asked whether placing a child with Darrell's limitations would be difficult. With all honesty, Mr. Davis had to say that finding a family willing to take on the financial and emotional burdens of rearing him would be tough. He explained that he was applying for SSI (Supplemental Social Security Income) benefits for Darrell so that the boy would be more "attractive" to potential adoptive parents.

In his report of his home visit, Mr. Davis made notes that Marge watched Darrell like a worried mother hen. She made sure he stayed away from anything potentially harmful, while she allowed him freedom to explore. Mr. Davis recorded that Darrell was active, playful, and clean. This reflected positively on the foster parents. Although Darrell did not walk, he was surprisingly mobile. His foster parents had difficulty explaining that Darrell could say only "mamamama" and "da da." They suspected that he might be retarded mentally as well as developmentally. Marge interjected that the doctors weren't sure whether he had a speech defect rather than retardation. She asserted that if the people who adopted Darrell didn't actively work with him, "he will dry up to nothing."

Darrell now was in special-education and early-childhood development classes and received most of his therapy at school.

After the half-day program the older children and foster parents continued his therapy.

* * * * *

Christmas of Darrell's third year was marked by mild seizure activity. His medication was increased. Dr. Gibson now assessed that Darrell's brain damage was more severe than the doctor had thought originally. Even with all of the intervention his cognitive development was progressing extremely slow.

Soon after the New Year, Marge and Joe were pleased to learn that Darrell's birth parents' rights had been terminated. Criminal charges of child abuse still were pending. After the termination hearing Darrell's parents refused to attend a "good-bye" visit. They said this would be too stressful on them. The Decree of Termination was signed and filed. The foster parents were relieved. No longer would the anxiety of weekly visits face them. They also no longer would worry that the birth parents somehow would have Darrell returned to them.

Anxiety was a part of their lives. Darrell's seizures began to worsen. In one five-minute period, Marge counted 21 minor episodes. A frantic phone call to Dr. Gibson permitted Marge to increase his medication. If this intervention did not cause the seizures to subside within 24 hours, Darrell would have to go to the hospital. Worried, Marge convinced Mrs. Harris to make a home visit that afternoon so that she could observe Darrell's behavior.

Marge held Darrell on her lap until she was sure he was stable. She then allowed him to get down on the floor. He walked a short distance into the kitchen and sat frog-legged on the tile floor. Suddenly he stopped babbling and playing. He leaned over and banged his head on a cabinet. Before he had time to fall farther, Marge jumped up, ran, and grabbed him up. She explained to Mrs. Harris that this was one of his mild seizures. The severity of the blacking-out and falling varied. Marge was emphatic that whoever adopted him constantly must watch him because, during the seizure, he lost all body control. If he was standing, he would merely fall over and hit his head or would fall on something that could injure him.

Darrell's seizures continued. One lasted eight minutes and worried Marge so greatly that she and Mrs. Harris rushed him to Dr. Gibson's office. Medication was changed again, but he was not hospitalized.

* * * * *

The criminal charges against Darrell's parents went to trial. Linda was found guilty as charged and was sentenced to 10 years probation. She received leniency since Crystal never had shown signs of abuse. The judge felt that Crystal was not in danger and that she should not be deprived of her mother. The judge ordered Linda to have no contact with any young children except her daughter. Dwayne was acquitted of all charges. The sentencing satisfied Marge and Joe, who waited at home for the verdict. They wanted Darrell's injuries vindicated, but they didn't want to see Crystal separated from her mother.

The elderly couple was devoted to Darrell. They spent hours agonizing and praying over his best interests. They desperately wanted to adopt him themselves and thought that they should be considered as a last resort. Darrell needed younger parents who had good medical insurance. Marge and Joe's other adopted kids now were in their teens. Their own children were grown and had families of their own. If Marge and Joe were to adopt Darrell, they would be in their late 70's when he graduated from high school.

Another big factor in their decision was the fact that Darrell's birth family lived in the same small town as did Marge and Joe. This caused stress to the older couple. Occasionally when they shopped, they would see Grandmother or Linda. Each person ignored the other and went in opposite directions.

Linda and Grandmother couldn't suppress their animosity. Marge harbored a sense of guilt for having someone else's child.

Just in case other parents couldn't be found, Marge and Joe submitted an application to adopt. With relief and anxiety, they accepted the news that someone had applied to adopt Darrell, now three-and-a-half years old.

EIGHT

Promise of Wisdom

"If any of you lacks wisdom, he should ask God, who gives generously . . ." (Jas. 1:5).

As I held little Nick on my lap, Bob Davis, Darrell's adoption social worker, turned to me. He handed me several thick notebooks containing case records and invited this prospective adoptive parent to look through them while we waited for other staff members to arrive. While I listened attentively, I quickly glanced at the photos. Bob briefly reviewed Darrell's birth history: born three-weeks premature, injured by his birth parents—probably by being shaken, a history of medical problems and seizures, and legally blind. He was progressing slowly in preschool intervention and therapy. Those bulging volumes, so condensed, left me with many unanswered questions

Darrell's teacher and therapists crowded into the small office, introduced themselves, and squeezed into the remaining chairs. They reported that Darrell was developmentally delayed in all areas, but they assured me that blind children are characteristically slow in developing measurable skills. Each teacher expressed a genuine love for this child. They each believed that he was near-normal in intellectual potential, even though he was not passing age-appropriate baby milestones. He was attentive, energetic, usually cooperative, and assertive. Most retarded children, they explained, were lethargic and complacent.

These children didn't care what happened around them. His frustration at not being able to communicate explained Darrell's tantrums. Each teacher described his strengths and was confident that he would continue to progress.

Although his speech consisted of only a few approximations of words, Darrell seemed to comprehend well and responded appropriately, when he desired.

Bob complimented me. They had selected my application for adopting Darrell because I was an experienced parent and teacher who could understand his needs. Even though I was single, I had a stable income with good health insurance. Now I had to decide whether I could accept the responsibilities of his care. They told me that Darrell's foster parents doted on him and were understandably upset about losing him. Because of their age and their responsibilities for their other children, the agency had not considered them as adoptive parents. I assured Bob that since I, too, had been a foster parent, I felt empathy for them and would be happy to stay in contact with them.

Nick and I followed in our car, as Bob led through a rural area to a lovely, large, brick, ranch-style home on the rise of a small hill. The sky had begun to darken and to cloud over. The wind was picking up as we parked on the drive and converged at the back door. Nick, distracted by puppies scampering on the lawn, did not enter the house with us when an older man ushered us into the kitchen.

I recognized Darrell from his many photos. The thin, blond little boy was perched on the hip of a grandmotherly woman, who held him protectively. Introductions were informally made. As Bob introduced me to Marge, I began to talk to Darrell, who was babbling and laughing.

Smiling to choke back a sob, Marge told Darrell, "Here. Go to your new mom."

She tried to hand him to me, but he wiggled to get onto the floor. I embraced her with a hug and patted her on the back. We were all too choked up with emotion to talk.

Nick broke the emotional strain by entering the kitchen. He stood behind me and stared at his new little brother, who was prancing in place, flapping his hands, and giggling. Darrell grabbed Marge's hand to pull her from the kitchen. Like ducklings we all followed into the family room. Darrell released her hand, plopped down, and "side-windered" across the room. He ignored us all and sat with the side of his face against the TV screen. Marge laughed as she explained that he liked to feel the vibrations and to hear the sounds of the TV. "But it sure is hard to see around him!" she exclaimed.

My first son hung back. He was confused by this strange little boy with whom he had hoped to play. Although Nick had watched the home video with me, I knew he had difficulty comprehending Darrell's behavior. I thought I was prepared. In reality, I wasn't. We listened as the foster parents related scattered memories of Darrell's young life—his likes and dislikes, his peculiarities. Two social workers, the foster parents, Nick, and I asked countless questions. Nick snuggled into Marge's heart when he climbed onto her lap to ask permission to explore a toy box. With her approval he contented himself with Darrell's toys and ignored Darrell.

Darrell danced over to Marge's rocking chair and climbed onto her lap. She hugged him while he squirmed and threw himself back and forth to make the chair rock faster. I tried to talk to him. His only response was active listening and the word, "Hi?"

Darrell wiggled down, appeared by my chair, and stood with his head cocked as he listened to me talk to him. His bright blue eyes did not focus. They made rapid little jerking movements as he stared in the direction of my voice. He climbed onto my lap and straddled it to face me. He took my hands and patted them together while he laughed and giggled.

Marge handed me a children's book. Darrell patted it furiously with both hands. Then he held it in his left hand. He pressed it against his left eye. Ignoring our attempts to talk to him, Darrell got down and swung the book in wide arcs across his body.

Nick crawled over on his hands and knees to be at Darrell's level. He silently tried to get the little boy to take a toy truck that he offered. Darrell ignored him. I encouraged Nick to talk to Darrell, but he just stared at him. We both would have to learn how to relate to him. Darrell flopped down, frog-legged, to rapidly scoot sideways toward a toy piano. Up he jumped and banged mercilessly on the keys. Marge commented, "To think that he once was so lethargic! Now he never stops."

I coaxed Nick to play the piano with Darrell. Nick began to bang, too!

"Nicky", I called over the din. "Get that ball with the bells inside it and see if Darrell will roll it back and forth to you."

This piano concert had to stop.

The kids' activities and our broken conversations had quickly broken the ice and cemented our friendship. We didn't realize that rain had begun until thunder and lightening startled us.

Saying a rapid "good-bye", we each rushed to our cars. Nick and I drove through boiling thunderclouds that blackened the sky. By the time we reached the motel, the storm was torrential.

By morning the storm passed. I called Marge and arranged a short visit with Darrell and his family before I began our long drive home. We were more relaxed now and met as old friends.

Reflecting on Darrell's development, I rationalized that at three-and-a-half years of age, he was mobile, could see well enough to get around, had a keen sense of hearing, and was inquisitive. His speech delay was not unusual for a blind child. Other developmental delays also were common with the blind. His hyperactivity could be because of the medications for seizures, or perhaps he was more intelligent and tried to satisfy his curiosity. I was elated that he seemed to have so much potential for continued development.

Nick slept most of the trip home, so my thoughts and prayers were not interrupted. I discovered that as I began to think about something specific, I began to pray about it. As I consciously prayed, I got sidetracked by another thought. Finally I learned that I could merely talk to God in a conversational way about whatever He brought to my mind.

This was not the way I had learned to pray, but as I talked to Him, I received answers that obviously were from Him. I knew that I did not have to have any formality.

* * * * *

A museum in our town hosted a special, interactive exhibit for children. The exhibit was on handicapped awareness. I took Nick to see what we could learn that would help us with Darrell. Nick rode in a wheelchair and then pushed me in it. We tried out several other activities before we reached a large wall that enclosed an irregular space. We chose from a rack of partial masks that would help us simulate various visual handicaps. Our first choices were masks that were completely light-proof. Donning our masks Nick and I followed the wall by trailing our hands along it. Nick rushed ahead. I tried to identify the surfaces that I touched. One part of the wall felt like brick; another felt like wood paneling; another section was carpeted. We found a section of chain-link fencing; another section had rough, cedar fencing. With tears hidden behind my mask, I reached the end of the wall. What could Darrell see?

While Nick played in the area, I tried another mask. This one was made of heavy, translucent—or foggy—plastic. Through the grayish light I could see faint color. Very large, dark shapes appeared, but I couldn't distinguish what the objects were. Is this what Darrell saw? How could I find out? Would the knowledge make any difference in his treatment or in how we treated him?

* * * * *

Our next trip to visit Darrell included a visit to Dr. Gibson, who still was Darrell's pediatrician. With straightforward answers he replied to my many questions. The doctor gave me added insight into cerebral palsy. Some of Darrell's jerky movements probably were caused by the brain injury. Cerebral palsy referred to paralysis or tremors that the brain's malfunction caused. The doctor explained that this "label" could help Darrell gain services as he grew older.

Dr. Gibson's opinion was that Darrell's developmental delays primarily were due to his being blind and not being able to relate normally to his environment. The doctor cautioned that he might have retardation. Dr. Gibson theorized that Darrell's tantrums occurred because the boy could not communicate with others.

Nick and I visited Darrell in his foster home and then took him to the motel. I was very apprehensive about caring for him alone. By the time Nick became bored with watching TV, I had decided to test my ability to deal with Darrell in public. Nick and I took him to a park with a playground. I put a body harness with a leash on him because he would not hold my hand without squalling. With his rapid, unsteady gait he ran into people and objects. The boys began to play in the sand. I felt a little more at ease until an older boy asked me why I had a "dog thing" on Darrell. This would be the first of many times that I made this explanation to a stranger: Darrell couldn't see.

Again I questioned my abilities. How could I protect Darrell from injuring himself? He did not fear heights or running into things when he danced around. Aware that people watched us, I was uneasy. When Darrell began to stamp up and down and flap his hands, Nick went to another part of the playground. Another child moved closer to stare at Darrell. I took a deep breath and told the boy that Darrell could not see. I explained that this is why he acted funny. The boy said, "OK", and was satisfied.

Adults stayed away as though he were contagious. I would need a while to adjust to this attitude.

We left the park to drive to a supermarket for a few things so we could eat a light supper in our motel room. I wasn't about to try a restaurant—not even for fast foods. As long as Darrell's shopping-cart carriage was moving, he was not too wild. Nick pushed, while Darrell giggled and kicked his legs. We had to steer down the center of the aisles to keep Darrell's swinging arms from contacting the merchandise.

As we brought our groceries back to the motel, I discovered that a residential neighborhood—just right for a walk— adjoined the back of the motel. Darrell rode in Nick's old stroller. He happily dragged his feet as long as we moved. When we stopped, he fussed and jumped around. Nick or I had to keep a tight grip on the handle of the stroller to keep it from tipping over.

Darrell wasn't interested in eating the baby food that Marge had provided. He refused the finger foods I had bought. He preferred to stand with his hands and the side of his face pressed against the window or the TV. I wanted to see whether Darrell liked a bath as much as we had been told. As soon as he heard the water running, he joined me in the bathroom. With help, he pulled off his shirt. He stepped on the heel of one of his shoes so he could wiggle his foot out. He repeated the process to remove the other shoe. Once his pants were dropped below his bulky diaper, he stepped on alternate pant legs and pulled his feet out of the pants. The diaper tape confused and frustrated him as he pulled on it. As soon as the diaper was loose, he pulled it off. Like a seal he slid over the side of the tub and into the warm water.

What fun he had! He slapped the water and slid up and down the length of the tub. He reminded me of a wet walrus. Nick removed his clothes to join the fun in the tub. Even with the shower curtain closed, the floor and bath rug got soaked. To get the boys out, I let all the water drain out. Nick got out, dried, and dressed. Holding a towel, I swooped Darrell up without warning. I gently tickled him to distract him while I got him dry, diapered, and dressed. I could tell from his grunts that he would have preferred staying in the water.

He refused a bottle and everything else I offered to eat. Sitting on the side of the bed, I rocked Darrell to sleep. I was not too surprised that he woke up several times during the night and demanded a bottle, since he hadn't eaten before he fell asleep. I suspected that the night bottles had become a habit. If Darrell took several bottles during the night, of course he would not be hungry during the day.

On our next weekend visit, without saying anything to Marge, I gave him only a bottle of water at night. He took enough to pacify himself and then went back to sleep. He seemed to eat better the next morning. I didn't tell Marge what I had done. She had struggled to keep Darrell alive because she was so protective of him and was miserable about losing him. She had done only what she thought was best for this skinny kid who didn't like to eat and wouldn't try to feed himself.

During the next couple of weeks, I took in two teen-aged foster kids—Grace and Simon. Both needed an immediate temporary placement. Darrell's adoption worker agreed that since Darrell was accustomed to older children in the home, this arrangement would not affect the adoption placement. As teens, they should be helpful, I hoped.

At the store, Nick discovered a huge, stuffed lamb. It had a soft, wooly texture and was adorable. He insisted that since Darrell could feel it, he would like it. The lamb had a small bell attached to a ribbon around its neck. Nick just knew Darrell would make it ring. I balked at the price but was so proud of my sensitive son that we bought it as an arriving-home give for his new brother.

Our next visit was to bring Darrell home. I still was very apprehensive. He required so much supervision and care. I wasn't sure I was up to it. My prayers and prayer-listening had convinced me that this was God's plan. I still had doubts. I tried to focus on faith—Faith with a capital "F." God would show me the way. Through Him I knew I could deal with anything.

I also was reluctant to say good-bye to Marge and Joe. I already had promised to send photos and letters and to bring Darrell back for a visit. I extended an open invitation for their family to visit us. We had exchanged mailing addresses and phone numbers.

Darrell's clothing and toys were packed in the back of my van. We gave and received hugs all around; then, in tears, Marge rushed inside the house. My new son was enthroned in a new car seat in the back between Grace and Nick. I gave Joe one last hug, wiped tears from my eyes, and turned my back to get into the driver's seat. I backed out of the driveway and then turned slowly onto the country road. Tears streamed down my face. I felt as though I were a kidnapper.

We stayed one last night in the motel, in a double room, so I could get some rest before the long drive home. We called for pizza delivery and then relaxed with TV as Grace and Simon got to know Darrell. I rocked a sleepy Darrell while I sat on the side of the bed with him straddling my lap. My back ached. At last he went to sleep. Exhausted with tension, concerned about my new role, and fearful of the huge responsibility I had taken on, I coaxed Nick onto a pallet on the floor. Simon went to his room. From her bed Grace watched TV. I stretched out beside Darrell. Previously I could end the visit and take him back to Marge if I felt overwhelmed. Now I was on my own. Only time would tell if the teens would be much help.

Darrell had only water during the night. He woke up hungry enough to feed himself dry cereal and part of a banana and to take a few sips of milk from a training cup. All of Marge's warnings concerning Darrell's being a poor traveler had prompted me to prepare snacks, toys, children's music tapes, and other diversions for the long trip home. The trip was less stressful than I anticipated, with Nick and the two teens providing distractions. We were off to a good start.

* * * * *

In his foster home, Darrell had begun to sleep in a crib. I didn't want to start him in a crib that he'd rapidly outgrow. I put him on a low, single bed pushed against the corner wall. I knew he could climb on and off easily. I hoped he would be happier than he would be confined to a baby bed. Darrell's room was entered through mine, so I could easily hear him. His room was stripped of anything that could hurt him. I had installed a gate across his door.

Our first night home he was tired and fell asleep quickly. I didn't. I stared at the ceiling and worried about our stairs, about feeding him, about my lack of sleep, and whether the other kids would get their fair share of my attention. The first time Darrell awoke during the night, I gave him a bottle of water to reassure him. I then patted his back until he fell asleep. The second time he woke, I quietly listened outside his door while he climbed on and off the bed. Within a short time he lay back on the bed and fussed himself back to sleep without a bottle and without a tantrum.

Thanking God profusely for conquering this obstacle, I tried to sleep. I dozed and dreamed of dangers that I vowed to fight for Darrell. He woke at daybreak to cruise the room. Seemingly he was content. I dozed until Nick jumped on my bed and begged to be allowed into Darrell's room to play. Confident that they wouldn't hurt each other or get into trouble, I dozed again and was aware that I could hear them playing happily.

Darrell accepted his new bed and new surroundings without the upset I had expected. He wandered around the downstairs of our house. He seemed inquisitive and felt his way. He was not at all disturbed by the unfamiliar. I removed a gate at the bottom of the stairs and watched. He negotiated the stairs under constant supervision but with no physical assistance. I held my breath. Gates would keep him off the stairs and out of some rooms when I was busy.

All of the outside doors had high locks installed. Darrell preferred being outdoors and could get most doors open. We had a large, enclosed porch with self-locking gates, so if he did manage to get outside, he was confined to the porch.

Summer vacation now was upon us. When they were not at work, my teen foster kids helped me with Darrell. Nick was a real blessing. He entertained Darrell as he kept an eye on him and helped me around the house. I had hoped for an age-appropriate playmate for Nick, but the differences in their personality and abilities brought out Nick's loving, compassionate nature.

My first goal was to do away with bottles. I thought that Darrell would develop an appetite and would eat better. I was anxious because his four upper teeth were decayed since he had sucked on a bottle at night. I dreaded a visit to the dentist. At meal times I gave him a variety of finger foods, placed his hands on the food, and encouraged him to pick up the pieces to feed himself. I offered other foods with a spoon.

Darrell already was using a sipper cup by himself without too much spilling. I never gave him a bottle again. He accepted this giant step of growing up much faster and with less fuss than I had anticipated. I felt successful and confident that my son would be normal.

We spent our first weeks of summer leisurely getting to know each other. Darrell usually entertained himself. He did not interact with anyone for very long. Two additional foster kids joined our family. The pre-teen sisters adored Nick and Darrell and were excellent in-house sitters. Except for brief periods of interaction, usually at meal times, Darrell ignored all of us.

We tried outings to the park. My extended family helped me keep an eye on Darrell as he flopped down in the sand to run his hands across the gritty surface. They followed as he wandered around. If other children were not around, we took turns encouraging him to climb the playground equipment. "Step up. Step up. Step down. Down." With his foot Darrell carefully felt for the steps. He was able to negotiate a few steps as he held onto the railing. We learned that he liked the swings. He wiggled his bottom onto the swing and hung on tightly while one of us pushed him. When he tired, he dragged his feet until the swing slowed and stopped.

Shopping trips were a disaster. Darrell would not walk and hold someone's hand. Unexpectedly he flopped down on the floor, screamed, knocked into things by swinging his arms, or grabbed some unsuspecting person's legs. Because Darrell's physical appearance was that of a cute, little boy, his erratic behavior drew negative attention from strangers, who assumed he was just a brat. Soon I resorted to a stroller with a harness to keep him from climbing out.

Darrell's first Sunday-school experience was an *experience* for all of us. The nursery workers were not prepared, although I had told them everything I knew. Darrell entered the classroom and plopped down on the floor. I stayed out of sight and hearing as I observed the teachers trying to engage him in age-appropriate activities. We all quickly agreed that since he was so small for his age and was developmentally delayed, the toddler class would be the best place for him. His new teacher was excellent for him. She let him wander around and didn't pressure him. If he got cranky, a cracker in each hand worked a miracle.

Our church did not allow children over three years of age to stay in the nursery during the worship service. Darrell was reasonably quiet during the song service. He cocked his head to listen. However, as soon as the music stopped, he began to squall and squirm. I quickly carried him back to the nursery. Again we agreed to consider him a toddler. My church friends encouraged me to leave him with them and to return to the service. I needed the spiritual refilling.

NINE

Seeking Professional Help

"Do not be anxious about anything, but in everything, by prayer and petition, with thanksgiving present your requests to God" (Phil. 4:6).

My kids enjoyed swimming in the neighborhood pool. Darrell no longer had tubes in his ears or ear infections, so I bought him a life jacket and introduced him to a big "bathtub." Darrell was ecstatic! He sat on the steps in the shallow end, slapped at the water, splashed, kicked, and giggled. He couldn't be happier. During the summer he invented his own games: jumping off the side, ducking his head, blowing bubbles, and trying to escape anyone who wanted to hold him.

My girls took turns watching him, so the daily excursions became less harrowing for me. I had opportunities to swim with Nick and by myself. When time arrived to leave the pool, I grabbed Darrell in a towel and calmly carried him, screaming and kicking, to the car. Fortunately the other regular swimmers soon got accustomed to Darrell and ignored his peculiar behavior.

The next step on my plan for young Darrell was to expose him to as many real-life experiences as possible so that he would develop some social skills. I wanted him to learn by expanding his environment. I hoped he would not throw tantrums in public. What I learned was to adapt to Darrell. He seemed unable to absorb and assimilate the stimuli we consider normal society. His tantrums in public did not decrease. He was not able to associate new experiences with familiar routines. After our initial move home, any activity or location that was unfamiliar caused him a great deal of stress.

Another step in my plan was to explore all medical treatments possible for him. I had a brief copy of his medical history besides what I learned by talking to Dr. Gibson and Marge. Much still existed that I did not know about Darrell's medical history. I had good medical insurance, so we first made a well-child visit to a pediatrician to establish prescriptions for Darrell's seizure medication. The doctor was most understanding of Darrell's needs and sympathetic of my desire to know what could be done for him medically. She made referrals for visual and hearing exams and for a CAT scan.

* * * * *

My four-year-old son rode in a large stroller into the hospital and up the elevator to the auditory evaluation clinic. As soon as the stroller stopped moving, Darrell struggled and squawked to get out. We got quicker service, I'm sure, than if he had been complacent. A receptionist ushered us into a smaller waiting area, where Darrell could be allowed out of the stroller, but he tantrumed anyway. I had no other place to take him, so I sat with him standing between my knees. I restrained him as I bear-hugged my arms around him and pinned down his arms. He tried to bite me. He had a lightning kick in any direction, so I wrapped my legs around his legs. He screamed and fought. If an arm or leg wrenched from my grip, he kicked out at the furniture and people or grabbed and pinched anyone within reach.

Ignoring stares, I talked to him more calmly than I felt. "Darrell, calm down, and I will let you go", I said, as I tried to talk him out of the tantrum.

Over and over I repeated, "Calm down." If he began to relax his struggles, I relaxed my grip. If he started struggling or screaming, I tightened the hug and covered his mouth, if I could free a hand from gripping his hands. I was very cautious and did not cover his nose or prevent him from breathing. By this time patients who hadn't left the room were giving me "dirty looks" if they had not witnessed the behavior leading up to restraining. Others were smiling in sympathy. As Darrell wore down, I loosened up gradually. As soon as he felt me relax a little, his tantrum intensified. This kept up until he finally gave up or was distracted. Then I could let him go. I rewarded his good behavior with a cracker or two.

At last a technician presented Darrell with a medicine cup that contained a sedative. Coaxing him to drink resulted in locked lips and spilled medicine. At my suggestion she drew the sedative into a large, needle-less syringe and squirted it into his mouth between his cheek and clenched teeth. Thirty minutes later Darrell was groggy but not yet asleep.

I carried him into a small exam room equipped with a rocking chair, a crib, and a bank of electronic equipment. I rocked Darrell, now snugly wrapped in a blanket, as he squirmed. He received another squirt of sedative. He went to sleep. I placed him in the crib, patted him on the back, and jiggled the crib. A technician tiptoed in to place earphones over his ears. He applied some salve to his head and attached electrodes to his skull.

I was instructed to pat his back and to keep him company. He must remain asleep while sounds were transmitted through the earphones. Somehow the electrodes would pick up his brain's response to the sounds he heard. When the test results were translated, the doctors would have a record of what he could hear. They would know if his hearing had any bearing on his lack of speech development.

Darrell would not stay asleep. The headphones were in place. The room was dark and quiet. I reassuringly patted his back. As soon as a sound was transmitted, he began to wiggle and reach for the earphones or electrode wires. I rocked him back to sleep by jiggling the bed. We pinned a blanket around him to keep his arms and hands still. He got loose. The audiologist called a pedi-neurologist to confer on another sedative. Darrell was given a different concoction. I returned with him to the rocker in the darkened room.

I almost fell asleep before he did. The technician crept in to whisper an offer to help me put him in the crib. Darrell squirmed and opened his eyes. Back to the rocker with all the lights off. Another lullaby. He sat straddling my lap and faced me with his head on my shoulder. I rocked and stroked his back until he finally slept again. I motioned to the technician to put the earphones on him while I continued to rock, hum, stroke, and pray that this time he would cooperate.

The technician quietly shifted equipment into position, hooked up the electrodes that had worked loose, and gently placed the earphones on him. I kept rocking and patting but no longer humming. Stiff from holding my position, my arms ached. Darrell's hearing test was completed at last.

A couple of weeks after our ordeal I received the test results. The doctors reported that Darrell's hearing was normal. It did not relate to his lack of speech.

The medical information I received from CPS left questions as to what Darrell actually could see. A visit to a pedi-optometrist was an easier ordeal than was the audiologist's exam because I was better prepared. I went equipped with crackers, a drink, and toys. The waiting area had a well-stocked play area for children.

The optometrist was extremely patient as she used a pen light to look into Darrell's eyes. He sat on my lap and tried to grab the light beam. I had to restrain his flying hands without sending him into a tantrum. Fortunately the doctor was experienced with kids and was blessed with understanding. Her brief exam confirmed blindness because of optic nerve atrophy. The optic nerve looked "pale", she said. His eyes were healthy and receptive, but the visual images were not getting through to his brain. Since the doctor could not test how well his brain processed the visual images it received, she willingly made referral for additional testing.

Nystagmus caused his eyes to jump or flutter. This affected his ability to focus. The doctor confirmed my suspicions that Darrell had almost no functional vision in his right eye. To my dismay no surgery could improve his sight. My prayers for a miracle had not been answered, but I received some hope that Darrell could be trained to use his limited vision. We discussed encouraging him to be left-handed to take advantage of the limited vision in his left eye.

I made an appointment for a visually stimulated brain scan to determined what visual input his brain actually received. This exam was as exhausting as the auditory exam had been. I had crackers, toys, and some children's books, but Darrell needed to be sedated this time, too. Again he refused to go to sleep. We sat in a darkened room, where I tried to rock him. When he was groggy, I sat with him on my lap as we faced a TV monitor. My arms were wrapped around his arms and hands. My legs enveloped his legs. Electrodes were taped to his skull again. Wires trailed everywhere.

The vision technician gently held up Darrell's left eyelid while the TV screen displayed a variety of changing patterns. At first the patterns were black and white. Then several shades of gray were introduced. The patterns flashed on and off at different rates. Colored patterns replaced the gray ones. The whole process was repeated while the technician held up his right eyelid. She then attempted to repeat the process and the whole sequence of patterns while she held open both eyelids.

Although the procedure was not complicated, Darrell's behavior was so uncooperative that we had a physical struggle to keep him from pulling the wires loose and getting away from us. The technician tried the tests over and over. Even groggy, he wiggled his hands loose from my bear hug again and again. I bribed him with the last of the crackers, but then he started to squall. The frustrated but patient technician could have given up, but the compassionate young woman withdrew a bag of chips from her own lunch to bribe him so she could finish the tests.

She ran out of chips. He reached the end of his endurance. I was exhausted and ached from restraining him. She and I were stressed out. For more than an hour the entire clinic had been upset by his yelling, so she disconnected his wires. I let him get down. She carried him to a soft-drink machine and bought him a canned drink. As soon as his stroller started moving, Darrell fell into a sound sleep. The technician and I glanced at each other. Could he have been tested while he was in the stroller?

Results from the visual exam were worth the anxiety and stress. I learned that with his left eye Darrell could see color and light-and-dark contrasts. He had very limited depth perception because he did not have use of both eyes. He seemed to have "blind spots" that were not always in the same place. This would account for the times he ran into things that previously he had avoided. It might explain how he could pick up small objects off the floor.

A special-education diagnostician for the local school district gave Darrell development tests. At age four he was functioning at the cognitive age of about 20 months. We agreed to place him in a nearby rehabilitation center for severely handicapped children. Darrell and I visited the school in late August. I instinctively felt positive about the environment and staff. I especially was heartened after I saw the indoor pool. I conferred with the teachers and therapists and watched their interaction with Darrell and the other children. I believed that this facility was qualified to meet his educational and physical needs. Another prayer had been answered.

Although Darrell had had many tantrums during that summer, the incidents often seemed to be predictable but unavoidable. He hated to wait or to stop moving. He could not be still in a chair or at the table except to eat. He did not like to be physically confined. His favorite object was an old magazine that he patted and flapped or deliberately put on his lap, a table, or the floor so he could rub his hands rapidly across its surface.

On his first day of school I was jittery and apprehensive. I had talked to the bus driver on the phone but had not met her. We waited at 6:30 in the morning for the special-services bus to pick up Darrell. With the other children in school and my teaching schedule I could not take him to school, even on his first day. He returned at 4 p.m. The driver, Tina, got off the bus with Darrell to talk to me. Meeting Tina, I knew he was in good hands. She had assigned him a toddler's seat by a window and had a supply of old magazines and crackers to keep him occupied. She told me a little about her other students. Some of these kids were in wheelchairs; some were mobile. All were profoundly handicapped in one or many ways. Most were retarded in mental development as well as having severe physical challenges.

Tina and I became immediate friends. She had patience with her young charges but would not tolerate misbehavior that she knew they could control. On the bus she had a radio tuned into a music station. With crackers and his books, he usually was willing, after a brief struggle, to accept his car-seat harness. I knew he would be in excellent hands. Therefore, I could return to my teaching.

I continued to try to give Darrell exposure to new experiences in places in which his noisy, hyperactive behavior would be tolerated. We could go to the mall only if Darrell was strapped in the stroller and if someone was constantly making it move. A grocery-cart seat proved acceptable as long as someone was pushing or jiggling. My foster kids were excellent help.

Someone offered my family tickets to a baseball game. Armed with crackers and drinks we gave the outing a try.

Darrell liked the noise and laughed and flapped his hands. He traveled between my lap and the laps of my other kids until his activity wore us all out. We left early. No one cared that the game was tied.

Our first experience at the circus was less successful. Our bleacher seats were on the railing several rows up. We stationed ourselves so Darrell had moving-around space. As long as we had lights, noise, music, and a lot of action, his behavior was okay. His tantrums were short because of a large supply of crackers and soft drinks. Darrell's rowdy, noisy behavior was verbally corrected. He was restrained when necessary but was not spanked.

I already was frustrated by his activity and squalling when a woman behind us loudly asked, "Can't you make that child behave?"

I turned around and tried to explain to her that he was handicapped. She cut me off and said that nothing was wrong with him that discipline wouldn't take care of. I was indignant and tried to ignore her self-righteousness.

We didn't stop going places, but now I was more prepared to offer excuses for Darrell's behavior to anyone who might be offended. I offered ready apologies. Without warning he might grab a woman around the leg or pat anyone on any part of his or her anatomy. His high-pitched squall could erupt at the most unexpected and most inopportune times. It was accompanied by kicking, head-banging, and frog-legged hopping.

Some of the most stressful trips for all of us were to the dentist. Well before Darrell's appointment, the dentist gave me a prescription to sedate Darrell. After our first visit to the waiting room, we were welcomed to enter by the back way. Darrell had four decayed "bottle" teeth that had to be pulled. Other teeth needed to be capped. We all sighed in relief when the ordeal of a series of appointments finally was over.

Darrell behaved reasonably well in school, where most of his day was spent in physical, occupational, and speech therapy. He was in a class of five multiply-handicapped and retarded children, with a teacher and an aide. Each child received therapy that the different specialists designed specially for him or her. Darrell was the most mobile of the children. With an attendant and a life jacket, on most days Darrell was able to play in the indoor, heated pool.

Of all the children, Darrell had the greatest number of tantrums. Reflecting their training and dedication, his teachers dealt with him calmly. As the violent behavior intensified, however, his tantrums became dangerous for the other children. He hit his head on the floor, thrashed around, and kicked out at anyone nearby. Adults could get out of his way, but the less-mobile children could not. The teachers worked out a "time out" by placing him, screaming and kicking, into a carpeted barrel. The barrel was as high as his shoulders so he could not get out, turn it over, or get hurt.

When I first learned about this type of discipline, I was upset, because Darrell hated to be confined. I soon realized that this method could work for that very reason. Although he required much longer than a normal child would to figure out that when he quieted and was not having a tantrum, the teachers immediately took him out of the barrel, he did learn. I could see that I actually was doing the same thing by wrapping my arms and legs around him and holding him tightly until he calmed down.

I often wished I had a "time-out" barrel at home. Many months later the teachers transferred the "time-out" concept so that they could send Darrell to a quiet corner of his classroom to be ignored until he calmed down. He always was kept under close observation. Many years later he learned to heed a warning of "time-out." Sometimes. This only worked if we could circumvent the actual tantrum. The difficulty was foreseeing a potential upsetting situation in time.

Tina, his bus driver, kept me informed of behavior at school. She made sure his car seat was by a window, that he had his beloved books or magazines to pat on, and that he had crackers. Tina and her assistant patiently waited out the first weeks of tantrums and turned up the radio until Darrell became familiar with the routine. He finally realized that he could not get out of his seat harness. He began to doze when the bus moved.

At home Darrell had the run of the house except for the bathrooms, where he liked to play in the toilets. He preferred the outdoors, so we had to remember to keep the doors locked. One cold, rainy, winter morning, I couldn't find Darrell in the house. The back door was open. In a panic, I called his name and ran outside looking for him. He was sitting in the largest water puddle in the driveway. He happily splashed the freezing, muddy water all over himself. I waded in after him to pull him to his feet. His screaming protest alerted Nick, who went to the door. When Nick stopped laughing at us, he went inside to search for a large towel and extra clothes.

Out on the porch, I stripped Darrell of his dripping sleepers and diaper and then bundled him into the towel for a quick run to the bathtub. The warm bath quieted him. How I laughed and anguished! I hoped that he would not associate sneaking outside to play in the puddles with his favorite activity—bathing.

* * * * *

Darrell's adoption could not be finalized until he had lived with me for at least six months. Our adoption worker made weekly, then monthly, home visits to evaluate his placement. I honestly shared with her my concerns and frustrations. He was not maturing mentally, emotionally, or socially, nor did he give any indication of being ready to potty train. I agonized over the tremendous responsibility, energy, and time this special child was demanding of me and my family. I could not give up on him. I assured the worker that I wanted to keep Darrell. I was prepared to be legally responsible for him. I conferred with my attorney. The paperwork was begun.

Another six months passed before we finally received a court date. For finalization, Darrell, Nick, and two of my foster kids and I went to the family law center and met our worker and the lawyer. An *ad litem* attorney had been assigned to represent Darrell, but the man never had met with us. Now, in the crowded, upstairs hallway, we waited for this lawyer to arrive. Darrell was not on his best behavior. A hectic hour later the lawyer still had not arrived, so my attorney asked the court for a delay. The *ad litem*'s office assured us that the attorney was on his way to court.

Darrell was not waiting patiently. He refused to stay in his stroller or on my lap. The other kids tried all their tricks to distract him. He screamed, danced around, swung his arms, grabbed at people, and refused to cooperate. He ate all of my supply of crackers.

I hoped a bailiff would talk to the judge or kick us out of the building. Officials told us that we could not leave the hallway. We had to be ready to enter the courtroom at a moment's notice.

Our worker took Nick and went to find vending machines to restock our snacks. We left our assigned bench to move to the end of the hallway so we would be less in the way. My kids and I took turns walking to the restroom and water fountain. After an additional two-hour wait, we all were exhausted from trying to distract and entertain Darrell while we endured the hard, wooden bench.

My attorney approached the judge to appeal that he hear our case without the *ad litem*. By now the judge had received reports about the little boy who was terrorizing the halls. He agreed to hear our case next. We moved our entourage to a bench outside the courtroom doors. We heard our case called. I swooped Darrell up in my arms to present him to the judge. In a matter of minutes Darrell legally was my son.

Our worker, by now a very dear friend, and I took the hungry kids to McDonald's to celebrate. Exhausted and full of crackers, Darrell fell asleep in his stroller. I was pleasantly surprised when my attorney, by now also a good friend, charged me only court costs. He, too, had fallen under Darrell's enchantment.

* * * * *

The second year that Darrell was a part of our family, we were invited to take him and the other kids to an Easter-egg hunt at the Lighthouse for the Blind. Volunteers had placed 9-volt batteries connected to beeping devices inside plastic eggs. The many blind children, helped by their parents, siblings, and volunteers, had a great time relying on sound to locate the eggs. A local newspaper reporter selected Darrell and several other children for a photo feature. How excited we were to see his handsome little face, hands cradling an egg, as a photo feature in the newspaper!

* * * * *

The summer that Darrell celebrated his sixth birthday, he had a CAT scan. Even with my advance warnings, the technician had difficulty sedating him. I held Darrell, rocked him, fed him, and sang to him. He refused to relax and to sleep. He received more sedative. Finally, he slept. I carried him to the exam room, carefully laid him on the CAT-scan table, and tiptoed out of the room to wait.

Once inside the machine, its clicks woke him up enough that he wiggled. Out they brought him. I patted his back and sang him back to sleep. Into the machine went the table. The clicks started again. He wiggled. Out the table emerged. The technician explained that Darrell had to be perfectly still for the CAT tests to be accurate. I smiled to myself. Darrell? Still? I repeated the back-patting and humming while he lay on the table, snoozing. The technicians conferred with a neurologist, who tried a different sedative.

This sedative helped Darrell to sleep soundly so that the personnel completed the tests. Results of the scan confirmed the damage I already knew about—the damage to the occipital lobes. No indication existed for a reason why Darrell was unable to learn to talk. All our efforts were futile. The CAT scan did not give us any new medical information.

* * * * *

The autumn of Darrell's sixth year, I met the mother of a boy—about Darrell's age—who had cerebral palsy. Little Mark received therapy at the same facility in which Darrell went to school. Mark was entering kindergarten at the school where I taught art to first- through third-graders. My principal, who was sympathetic to all children's needs, brought Karen and Mark to visit me in my classroom. Thanks to the principal's concern, Karen and I quickly became friends as we compared and contrasted the needs of our special kids. She told me about a horseback-therapy program in which her son participated. The program was designed to increase his sense of balance. An avid horse lover, I was intrigued.

Early one Saturday morning, Darrell, Nick, my two foster daughters, and I met our new friends at a beautiful facility—the Hope Arena—at Moody Gardens in Galveston. The director of the horseback-therapy program explained that the rhythmic motion of riding a horse often helped improve the balance of stroke victims, persons with cerebral palsy, and those with head injuries. The rider's body relaxed and swayed with the horse's walking gait. The relaxing and swaying strengthened muscles and aided balance. The riders gained an added emotional benefit of feeling in control of such a large animal.

Darrell qualified for a 30-minute session once a week for a token fee of only $5 per session. We signed up. The girls and Nick walked with Darrell up and down the spacious barn and played in the hay. They petted the inquisitive noses of the gentle horses housed in large box stalls. The barn was immaculate. Volunteers raked the stalls, brushed horses, and helped with the sessions.

I am an experienced rider. When I was much younger, I raised and trained horses. I was most curious and excited about this unusual program. The staff members allowed me to work with them and with Darrell as long as I didn't talk when he rode. If he heard my voice, he wouldn't pay attention to the staff.

A large, specially trained pony was cross-tied in the barn's alley. A volunteer placed a brush in Darrell's hand. She guided him to show him how to brush "his" horse's legs. She lifted Darrell so he could reach the horse's neck and head. The patient pony "woofed" through his nose. This sent Darrell into giggles. He dropped the brush, threw his arms around the pony's neck, and buried his head in the pony's mane. Like a puppy Darrell sniffed the horsey smell.

Trigger, a large, specially trained pony, was saddled with a bareback pad. He was led with a halter lead and positioned next to a mounting platform that was accessible by steps and a wheelchair ramp. Over several sessions the workers taught Darrell how to climb up the platform, pet the pony's head, locate the pony's back, and to mount with assistance.

One person—usually me—led the pony, while two "sidewalkers" walked by Darrell's legs. These helpers told Darrell to sit straight and encouraged his balance. Off we would go at a sedate walk. Darrell loved the swaying motion. He rubbed the pony's mane between his hands and patted his neck. We continued therapy for many months until our demanding schedule and Darrell's growing lack of cooperation forced us to quit.

An added benefit to going to Galveston for riding therapy was the beach. After each session, weather permitting, we joined Karen, Mark, and her younger son, Kris, on the beach for a picnic and a splash! Darrell was in heaven! Water still was his favorite activity. Even though his skin was pale, with coats of sunblock lotion he did not sunburn easily. We spent many relaxing Saturday afternoons with all the kids in the sand and water. We did this until autumn winds grew too cool.

* * * * *

Darrell had been granted SSI benefits before he was placed with me. These benefits had to be re-approved every year. To get this approval, I had to fill out a questionnaire. During Darrell's third year with me, the Social Security Administration questioned his eligibility. To substantiate his disabilities, I got updates on his school ARD (academic review and dismissal) reports and doctors' reports. I then submitted these to the regional Social Security office.

Officials required me to take him to the Social Security office. There they would interview us. Prepared for tantrums, I was well-stocked with crackers, books, and his stroller of toys. Confined in the small, crowded waiting room, Darrell had several classic tantrums. I think the personnel called us into the interviewer's office a little more quickly than they did others who waited. In the interviewer's cubicle, so we could talk, I tried to bribe him with crackers and to restrain him to calm him. He didn't cooperate. This upset the nearby personnel. The interviewer made notes as he tried to follow his standard questions about Darrell's handicaps and my income. He was certain that Darrell, because of his special medical needs, did qualify to continue receiving SSI benefits.

Imagine my surprise when I received a Social Security letter asking me to make an appointment with a particular psychiatrist! I had left the Social Security office confident that Darrell's retardation was apparent to the entire staff.

We made the appointment. The doctor was knowledgeable and friendly. She was not upset by Darrell's behavior. She tried to give him some basic cognitive tests and readily admitted that my seven-year-old son could not perform as well as a two-year-old could. He could not stack blocks, draw a line, or sit still for someone to read to him. He could not carry on a conversation and could only mimic a few sounds and say "Mamamaaa." He was not potty-trained. The psychiatrist's statement was that he was moderately retarded. I agreed with her. His teachers had been more optimistic and insisted that even though he was quite "slow", he was making some progress.

* * * * *

The next school year Darrell had a new teacher to whom he took an intense dislike. The well-trained, experienced young man treated him well, but Darrell's lack of cooperation and resulting tantrums convinced us to move Darrell to another teacher's classroom. None of us ever saw this extreme, negative behavior with the other men who worked with Darrell or with the female staff. No one could figure out this problem, so we just accepted it. The sensitive male teacher quietly avoided all contact with Darrell.

Darrell's behavior began to deteriorate, especially in public. His medication was adjusted, changed, and increased, to no avail. We used a larger stroller with a seat belt until he tore up the belt. His legs were long enough that he could drag his feet as we pushed him. At times he became so violent, throwing himself back and forward, that he threw himself and the stroller over backward.

God had provided my family with a series of babysitters—friends from my church—who were willing to deal with Darrell at home, where his behavior was more predictable and manageable. Now Darrell was excluded from many family activities and outings at which his behavior would cause problems. My other children, especially Nick, lovingly defended Darrell and hated for him to be left out. As Darrell grew older and his behavior more deviant from normal, the more his strangeness became an embarrassment to us all.

During this time, Darrell's teachers began to be concerned about episodes of strange behavior that seemed like mild seizures. He would sit frog-legged, press his hand against his eye, and not respond. At other times he leaned forward and repeatedly hit his head on the floor. Medical personnel took his blood levels and adjusted his medication, but the behavior continued. The teachers suggested autism. By calling his name or by touching him when he "spaced out", I always could get some response from him. To me an autistic person could not easily be distracted and returned to reality. We agreed, just now, not to add to his evaluation the label of autism.

* * * * *

To control his seizure disorder, medical personnel periodically had to draw Darrell's blood to evaluate the proper dosage of medication. The nurses, doctor, and I developed a procedure to accomplish this difficult task. On the examination table the nurse lay an opened papoose restraint. I carried Darrell into the room and lay him back on the padded restraint while the nurses wrapped him up and strapped him down. Of course he knew that something was up. He reacted violently—kicking, thrashing, and screaming. I lay across his chest and held his head. Another nurse held his arm and placed the tourniquet. A third nurse drew the blood. Darrell shrieked, tried to bite, and struggled to get loose. The process was painful for all. The whole office dreaded our visits. Once the personnel completed the procedure, I carried him around like I would a small baby and tried to comfort him.

On one of our visits, the pediatrician could hear Darrell's beginning tantrums upsetting the waiting room. Darrell was like my dog that could sense the vet's office. I could tell by the doctor's head shake and resigned smile that she dreaded another one of Darrell's tantrums in her office. She used tongue depressors to try to pacify him. She let him play with the curly cord on the blood-pressure cuff. As we tried to corral him, she performed her examinations in minute segments. He thrashed around the small exam room. The doctor then asked why I didn't use a wheelchair for him, since he had outgrown and destroyed the largest stroller I could find.

I answered that I couldn't afford one, nor did I think that Darrell would qualify for one because he was mobile, when he wanted to be. She immediately wrote a prescription for a wheelchair. He needed it for self-protection. I needed it for my sanity.

Since processing the paperwork would take time, I contacted the rehab center and borrowed an old chair. The physical therapist agreed that this was a good idea. She worked with the wheelchair people helping to design foot restraint straps to prevent Darrell's kicking. She specified a chest harness to keep him from throwing himself forward in the chair like he had done in the stroller. His doing that had caused the stroller to overturn.

In public the new chair was a blessing. Now he was under physical control. Also, as long as he was moving, he was happy. Now the general public accepted him as a handicapped child rather than as a spoiled brat. We had a few things to learn. If he stopped moving for too long, or if the brakes weren't tight, Darrell could turn the chair over backward by suddenly throwing himself backward. My kids, acting as his pushers, stayed busy.

When Darrell was eight, we tried another trip to the circus. This time we used the wheelchair. Unfortunately our seats were not situated so that he could stay buckled into his chair. He visited several of our laps and then settled on mine as the show began. Sooner than I expected, crackers, drinks, music, and the lights had exhausted their effects on Darrell. He began to tantrum. I wrapped in a bear hug my arms and legs around him. He threw himself forward, then backward with such force that the back of his head hit my nose and mouth. I saw stars and cried out in pain. Fortunately an usher had witnessed the incident and rushed over to offer assistance. He picked up the screaming child and led me, my lip cut and bleeding, through a maze of back hallways. He led me to the first-aid station. In the dim light I hardly saw through tears that the pain caused. The first-aid personnel applied ice to my swollen lip, cheek, and the bridge of my nose. Darrell, sitting on the usher's lap, happily sucked on ice chips. When the pain subsided, the bleeding stopped, and I regained my composure, the usher carried Darrell and led me back to to our seats.

My rapid disappearance and my instructions for them to "stay put" worried my other kids. When we returned, their sympathy and understanding encouraged me. Perhaps afraid of another incident, they offered to leave early. Nick strapped Darrell into his chair. The kids took turns pushing him down the ramps into the van. They didn't blame Darrell or get mad at him for ruining their outing. In understanding his limitations and in their compassion, they were wise beyond their years.

TEN

Thank God for His Helpers

". . . no eye has seen, no ear has heard, no mind has conceived what God has prepared for those who love him" (1 Cor. 2:9).

By 1989, I was a single parent with nine adopted children. When Darrell's prognosis seemed positive, my adoption worker had approached me about adopting additional children. By that time my foster children were adults and no longer needed me. I still harbored the idea of finding a brother for Nick, so I was open to an additional adoption. Instead of another brother, two sisters roughly his age joined Nick. My youngest daughter, aged seven, quickly became Darrell's second mom. A year later, Nick gained three brothers and a sister.

These kids had faced abandonment, abuse, and foster care, as well as the turmoil of settling into a new home. I was gratified that they accepted Darrell and his peculiarities. I didn't understand how this happened so quickly. Each child had asked questions about him and then stayed aloof for a short time. Before long, though, each one had defined his or her relationship with little brother. The boys tried to engage him in play. The girls delighted in mothering him. How I prayed that adults could be as accepting as these children were!

Darrell's strength and agility were unusual. With either foot, he could kick out in any direction. He often pinched hard enough to bruise and bit to draw blood. His violent behavior often was unexpected and unpredictable. No matter how well prepared I thought I was, his tantrums occurred at the most inopportune and embarrassing times. I stopped taking him to the other children's school functions because they were having a difficult time accepting and explaining to friends their little brother's behavior. Teens and an older woman from my church were willing babysitters. This really blessed me.

After the circus incident, I rarely took Darrell out in public except to the church nursery. Here, too, he began to get out of control. My attempts during the casual evening services to get him to listen to the singing before I took him to the nursery finally deteriorated into not taking him into the sanctuary at all.

To calm Darrell, our pediatrician tried several medications for hyperactivity. She suggested an MRI exam to compare with the old CAT scan. Perhaps she could learn something new.

On our first visit Darrell could not be sedated at all, so I rescheduled. At home, before the second appointment, I gave him a sedative, so he was groggy when we arrived. Medical personnel gave him another dose of the sedative and mummy-wrapped him on the MRI table. I whispered to him and tried to keep him calm. Slowly they inserted the table into the machine. The technicians took their places; the machine began to buzz. Then it clicked and made more strange noises. Of course, Darrell started to wiggle.

Out he emerged. The medical personnel gave him more sedative and re-wrapped and prepared him for the long, cylindrical tunnel of the MRI machine. The technicians whispered and teased me that I would have to go inside with him. Again the noises inside the tiny opening in the huge cylinder startled him. They pulled him out. The staff decided unless I was willing to ride in with him and to try to keep him still, they would have to give up the tests.

Knowing the tests results might help treat Darrell, I agreed to try. Fortunately I am not claustrophobic and was not too overweight, because the fit was extremely tight. I partially lay over Darrell with my right arm extended alongside his head, so I could rest my head on the arm. My left arm rested as lightly as it could on his chest, so that I could stroke him. I faced the side of his head, close to his ear. The movable table slowly began to slide into the tunnel. It stopped abruptly so a technician could tuck a sheet closer around my legs and make sure none of my larger body parts would hit the sides of the machine. The tubular machine felt like a sausage casing as we were stuffed inside. The walls were just inches away and surrounded our entire bodies.

When the clicking and whirring noises started, I was more startled than Darrell was. Inside the machine was much louder than when I stood outside. I patted him gently. I was cramped and very uncomfortable. He slept. About 20 minutes (or was it hours?) into the procedure, he started to stir. I whispered to him to keep him still. He worked one of his hands loose. They pulled us out. The technician teased me that I had made him wiggle to get out of there. I got off the table to stretch while they gave Darrell some more sedative and re-wrapped his restraints. In we went again. Shortly the noises stopped. The tests were completed.

A pedi-neurologist reviewed with me the MRI results. From the CAT scans we already knew about the scarring found in the occipital lobe of his brain. Small pockets that either were fluid-filled vacuum areas or small cysts were discovered in the frontal lobes. The CAT scan had not shown this. Unless these areas were to enlarge, the doctor did not think this was serious. The affected areas did control his ability to speak. Now we knew that brain damage because of the shaking injuries was causing Darrell's lack of speech development. Surgery or draining of these areas was possible but very dangerous. The doctor would not consider either unless something changed significantly. We arranged to have the hospital release Darrell's old CAT scan results so we could make additional comparison.

Nick pushed Darrell's chair through the corridors of the hospital to the x-ray records department. My kids and I began a long wait while personnel searched the files for his records. To entertain Darrell, I handed him a large, empty, manila mailer with a small, plastic window. As I talked to the receptionist, Darrell played with the mailer. He slapped it against his head and the chair arms and finally tore the mailer.

I directed my attention to the clerk. Suddenly one of my kids yelled out that Darrell was choking. I stood behind his chair and at first couldn't see his face. I called for help as I undid his chest harness. He gagged and struggled. His face turned bluish; his eyes bulged. He was petrified. So was I. Two interns heard the commotion and rushed over. One lifted Darrell high enough out of the chair to do the Heimlich maneuver as the other intern swept his mouth. The intern pulled out a long, plastic strip covered with bright blood. The strip was the "window" from the mailer.

My heart pounded as I thanked everyone. My kids blamed themselves for not watching him more closely. I reassured them that they were in no way negligent. Darrell was not in the habit of chewing paper or of putting things in his mouth. The accident happened. No one was at fault.

Driving home I relived the incident and shuddered. I prayed silently and thanked God for having people available to help Darrell. What if this had happened at home when he was out of my sight? We still must care for Darrell, at eight years old, as though he were an infant.

ELEVEN

Painful Decisions

"I always thank God for you because of His grace given you in Christ Jesus" (1 Cor. 1:4)

When I was 12 years old, I gave my life in special service to the Lord. We were in a youth conference during an altar call after the final service. Emotions were high. Without a doubt I knew that, a few years before, I had asked Jesus into my heart and life. At first I did not understand what the Lord compelled me to do. That night through prayer He revealed to me, amidst hundreds of teen-agers, that He had plans for my life that included children. I followed His call to become a teacher. Deep down I knew that rearing someone else's children was a part of that plan.

I taught Sunday school and Vacation Bible School and volunteered at the YWCA. After marriage and the births of my two daughters, children flocked to our house. Although my marriage failed, the Lord gave me strength to rear my daughters alone while I completed a degree to become a teacher. In the school setting, kids burdened with problems drew me to them.

I remembered Mark, who rode a mechanical scooter from class to class; Shawn, who was so blind behind his thick glasses that he drew with his head resting on his arm; Callie, who had Spina Bifida and was bent double in her wheelchair;

Brandy, who had Down syndrome, and Lydia, who was being blinded by glaucoma.

I began working with kids who had emotional problems. I remembered five-year-old David, whose mother took his twin sister and left him with his father and grandparents. Soon after, his beloved grandfather passed away, his dad left for an out-of-town job. In the classroom David's anger erupted in violence. I remembered Rusty, who was in his own world of autism and muteness. One of my first foster children was an 11-year-old girl who was pregnant because of incest. The year before she had been my student. The Lord was preparing me for His plan.

* * * * *

Now, seated with the envelopes from the Texas Department of Human Services, I tore open the top bulging mailer and extracted copious notes in doctors' illegible scrawls. After flipping through the stack of incomprehensible papers, I stuffed them back into the envelope. The second and third mailers contained copies of social workers' notes that were handwritten. They also contained neatly typed reporting forms. The final mailer contained copies of a mixture of forms and reports about Darrell's adoption. Overwhelmed by the minute details and volume of material, I hid the case study in my room until a better time presented itself.

With Darrell and the other kids asleep, I sorted the voluminous material into chronologically dated stacks that covered the kitchen table like sorted laundry. Randomly I picked up a stack and shuffled through it. I read whatever caught my attention. Tired and sleepy, I tried to memorize jumbled details of Darrell's young life.

With Darrell's case history on my mind, I attended his annual ARD meeting. The purpose of the meeting was to set goals for the next school year. His optimistic teachers agreed that he had made some progress—a few, tiny steps forward. I silently questioned whether their constant comparison to other retarded children limited their acceptance of reality. In reality, he did not have the mental capabilities for which we all had hoped. His vision was deemed adequate for close focus, but he could not match an object with a picture, or sort like objects, or work a three-object puzzle as well as a two-year-old could. Darrell said "mama" appropriately, although it usually emerged as a question. He said "eee" for eat, "kkk" for drink, an approximation of "car" meaning "let's go", and "buuu" for his favorite object—a book. His vocabulary had increased only by a few other word-sounds that he mimicked, without a contextual meaning. He had learned to make a limited number of hand-signs for the deaf. He did not initiate communication except by pulling on someone's clothing or by yelling. His tantrums at school increased in intensity with his growth and strength. He was not potty-trained. He was almost nine years old.

Through the post-adoption program my family had remained in close contact with Spaulding for Children. Our social workers had become family friends. Just after the ARD I contacted Darrell's worker and discussed Darrell's lack of development. Darrell simply could not function with the family outside of our home or school. The sitters who had been able and willing to deal with him were becoming less available and less willing. His worker and the staff had been concerned about Darrell's negative effect on the family and on my ability to cope. She assured me that she would help and support me if I decided to find a residential treatment facility for him. My heart would not consider sending him away from home.

* * * * *

Darrell grew larger and stronger. Even with increased medication his behavior continued to deteriorate. Everyone who loved him recognized that he needed 24-hour structure and 24-hour care that we could not provide. My other children's needs were not being met because of the stress of meeting Darrell's needs. With a heavy heart I began searching for a residential placement for him. I considered myself a failure. The hopes I had for rescuing this child and rearing him to be a productive member of society were dashed. I loved him dearly. I fought guilt and defeat.

Many nights I lay awake. I questioned God's purpose for bringing Darrell into my life and for continuing Darrell's life. What was the purpose of his existence? What about his future? I spent other late nights searching his old files for clues, answers, signs. I talked with my Lord without ceasing.

Reflecting in the mirror, I saw more gray hairs than black, dark circles under my eyes, and tell-tale signs that I was approaching middle age. My oldest daughters were married and lived in different states. My adopted kids were, one by one, metamorphosing into teen-agers and alternating between being civil and obnoxious. They all were in therapy to deal with issues of abandonment, neglect, abuse, and teen-age defiance. The stress of relating to each one's hormonal imbalance, personality, and past issues was exhausting.

Trying to allow logic to suppress emotions, I followed up a referral for Darrell to the Mental Health and Mental Retardation Association (MHMRA). Over the phone I explained Darrell's needs.

The agency gave us an appointment for an interview with an intake worker. Of course Darrell threw a screaming, kicking fit in the waiting room, so we didn't have to wait long. The personnel there interviewed us. They scheduled Darrell for a psychological evaluation, social study, and a home visit. I signed a release for school and therapy reports. They added to his file a financial report.

Months later MHMRA concluded that Darrell was a candidate for placement in one of its sponsored facilities. As soon as MHMRA completed the mountain of paperwork, the agency would begin searching for a facility that met his needs.

The MHMRA case manager who visited our home quickly became a friend. By now I had carefully read all four bulging mailers that contained Darrell's CPR, medical, and pre-adoption case files. I was even more convinced that placement outside of our home was in Darrell's best interest and in the best interest of the other children in my family. My kids did not agree with my decision. They could not understand the idea of sending Darrell away, even though they often suffered because of his tantrums. Their own experiences with abandonment and residential placements surfaced. I tried to convince them and myself that we were trying to help Darrell and not get rid of him. For several months I gathered the required information to complete an admissions packet.

* * * * *

I received a formal letter that set my heart racing. Social Security declared that Darrell had received more than $4,000 in SSI payments to which he was not entitled. The agency ordered me to repay the full amount or to appeal.

Of course, I appealed! To prove his handicaps I sent documents to Social Security. I reminded the office that its own psychiatrist had tested Darrell. Social Security had approved his eligibility. Neither adoption nor medical intervention had improved his condition. At last the agency dropped the case.

Darrell's behavior continued to deteriorate. He received Haladol in an effort to control his violent, destructive outbursts. He then became a lethargic zombie. After he went months with no improvement, doctors switched him to Thorazine. He seemed a little calmer and more aware. His tantrums became less frequent and a little less violent but were just as unpredictable and destructive. He had no self-control and no way to communicate. During each day he raged many times.

How I prayed that somehow we could discover what set him off! Was it a sound, a smell, or something of which only he was aware? If only we knew what upset him so much, we would do everything possible to pacify and appease him. To watch him suffer head-banging, lashing out, and throwing himself around on the floor was heart-wrenching.

At Easter the kids gave Darrell a cute, stuffed bunny that contained a music box. It operated by pressing on the bunny's heart. Darrell loved music and noise but was not usually fond of the texture of stuffed toys. We all thought that he would like this bunny. One of my kids touched the bunny's heart to start the music before he handed the toy to Darrell. Much to our surprise, Darrell began to sob. His lower lip quivered. He shrank back. His cry was not a tantrum but was a cry of despair and emotional pain. The kids and I glanced at each other in wonder and confusion.

Nick took the toy into another room and out of Darrell''s hearing. I hugged and consoled Darrell. I thought that perhaps the pitch of the music hurt his ears, although he did not act as though he felt physical pain. That evening Nick, not knowing that Darrell was in the next room, showed the bunny to one of the other kids. Nick pressed the bunny's heart. The music started. From the next room Darrell began to sob as though his heart were broken. I went in to him and held him close.

Nick hid the bunny and approached me. With tears in his eyes, he apologized to Darrell and to me. I hugged my sensitive son and assured him that what happened was an accident. With more wisdom than I possessed, Nick said that he thought maybe Darrell had heard that tune when someone had hurt him long ago. I had read theories about early-infancy memories that resulted from trauma, but I had discounted them. I now pondered the theory. Could this have happened in Darrell's infancy? Will we ever know?

We will never know so much: Darrell's purpose for living, what he thinks and feels, his contribution to society, his influence on others. I know he taught me patience and compassion to treat all people with God's love. I had learned to look at a special-needs child and speak directly to him. I could speak to parents with a reassuring, "I've-been-there" smile, and offer help.

My kids showed empathy and understanding as I dragged them along to Darrell's school, therapy, and doctors' appointments. They didn't shy away from the strange, misshapen, funny-looking kids they met. I prayed that their experiences would carry over into their adult lives.

* * * * *

In May MHMRA completed Darrell's evaluation and compiled everything into referral packets that it would send out to institutions that had possible future vacancies. I was comforted by that statement that finding a placement for a child with his needs could take years. That meant that I might have many months to prepare for separating from him.

His medical conditions included being blind due to hemiplegia, epilepsy, cerebral cysts, infantile cerebral palsy, and possible autism. He was declared to be profoundly retarded and to have an IQ of 36. The potential for mental growth for which doctors, social workers, therapists, teachers, and I hoped had not materialized. I was heartbroken at his "labels."

For emotional support I phoned my long-time friend, Karen. She reminded me that in my heart, I had known that Darrell was not progressing mentally, for at each ARD meeting for the past six years his goals had been a variation of the same goals for the year before. With this determination of profound retardation, he would be eligible for residential placement. I was devastated by the realization that Darrell never would become "normal."

I tried not to be angry with God for not "fixing" Darrell. Why did He bring this child into my life if I couldn't help him? Again and again I struggled with why God allowed this child to live, only to be a perpetual toddler.

With reluctance and despair I allowed copies of his common application and referral packages to be sent to several facilities that accepted children with his multiple handicaps. Personnel again cautioned me that a year or more could pass before a residence that could meet his needs would have a vacancy.

I confided to Karen that this wait would buy me time to prepare my other kids and myself for his move.

* * * * *

During the years of Darrell's deterioration and even with the additions to my family, I continued slowly working on a doctorate in education. Before my family grew so large, I completed my dissertation research study and then spent many distracted hours writing and rewriting for publication the conclusions. The entire graduate committee met my family, since my family members sometimes had to accompany me to brief meetings. Nick had enamored my major professor. I had started the graduate program before Nick was born. As an infant Nick occasionally attended classes with me. My committee allowed me an extension to complete degree requirements within the allotted time. In May of 1989 I was scheduled to receive an Ed.D (doctorate in education).

In the early spring of 1989 I received a letter informing me that I was one of several Houston-area persons selected to receive a Jefferson Award for public service. I was overwhelmed. I called the committee to learn that my second daughter, Colleen, had heard about the awards and had submitted a letter nominating me for my work with foster and adopted children. I immediately drove to Colleen's house to give her a huge hug. For years I had been concerned that she and her older sister, Cheri, had been jealous of all the attention the other kids received. Her expression of love humbled me.

The awards committee arranged for a TV reporter and camera crew to visit our family for video coverage they would show at the TV presentation of the awards.

The TV crew caught my kids interacting with Darrell as he rode our pony, Freckles. The kids rode their bikes and showed off. Darrell was on his best behavior. Each of us was interviewed. I tried to downplay myself—to emphasize the rewards of being a foster parent and an adoptive parent of special-needs kids. I wanted viewers to see as an encouragement our racially mixed, blended family.

In May my mom and all of my 11 children, except Darrell, attended my graduation exercises from the postgraduate school of the University of Houston. I received my doctorate of education degree. The TV station taped the graduation exercise and added it to the upcoming TV program.

The day of the Jefferson Awards, Colleen and I attended a banquet sponsored by the TV station. We met other recipients of the awards. The station aired the TV spot pre-recorded from our home and at my graduation. Later I received a video copy of the entire awards ceremony.

I never had thought about receiving rewards on earth for doing God's will. Since I was about 12 I had known that the Lord had called me to special service that involved working with children. Throughout my adult life, as I earned college degrees, reared my oldest daughters, and taught school, I remembered this calling. Needy kids constantly were in my path or on my doorstep.

As I became aware of "throwaway" teens needing a safe place to live, I knew God willed that I take in foster children. After I took in the pregnant 11-year-old, my home was licensed as a state foster home. Then God presented adoption. I did not search out a child. My first baby arrived in my home through the friends of my oldest daughter.

The Jefferson Award was an humbling experience and an opportunity to share with others what God had done in my life.

* * * * *

Spring, 1990. We began preparing for a family adventure. My cousin, a paleontologist, was conducting a dinosaur dig in Montana. He casually had extended an invitation to visit sometime. Little did he suspect that I actually would pack up eight kids and a teen-aged babysitter into a maxi-van that was pulling a pop-up camper to head north.

My kids and I began dreaming, planning, and dreading this camping trip. Two months before the scheduled June departure date, I received custody of my oldest adopted daughter's infant son, Chris. To our lists we added a car seat, stroller, baby backpack, diapers, and formula. Chris entered our hearts.

With Thorizine Darrell's behavior was somewhat under control. I strapped his wheelchair on top of the camper. We set off on a three-week trip through seven states and into Canada.

On the trip Darrell's body began to metabolize the Thorizine differently. He became lethargic. At times he was so sedated that he staggered when he walked. His behavior was more erratic than normal but was less violent. Fortunately he slept a lot while we drove. Although the road trip was much less stressful than I anticipated, I worried about him acting autistic.

Darrell tantrumed if we pushed his wheelchair too slowly or if we didn't have snacks readily available, but otherwise his behavior—for him—was good. On the return trip I was convicted that the Lord had calmed him down to allow us to have this family time together.

As a family adventure the trip was memorable. I have immortalized it in my other book, *Grandma's on the Go*.

In June we returned from our three-week camping adventure. I talked to Darrell's doctor about Darrell's strange reactions to the medication. Even though his behavior was more tolerable, we knew that the doctor had to adjust the dosage. If this medication could stabilize Darrell so that I could deal with him at home without his becoming a zombie, I would drop the process of institutionalizing.

Late in July Darrell's case manager with MHMRA called to arrange another home visit. She explained that the agency had sent his application packet to three facilities that accepted children with his handicapping conditions. She expected a six- to 12-months' wait for an available space. Meanwhile he would continue in year-around training at the rehabilitation center school.

The very next week I was shocked to receive another phone call from the MHMRA case manager. One of the facilities that had received Darrell's application had notified her that it had an opening. It would consider Darrell immediately. Was I interested? Whew! Yes? No! Questions scrambled my mind. I wasn't ready for him to leave our home so soon! Through my tears I fired questions. I wanted an excuse to not send him away. I was crushed by the urgency to respond as soon as possible. The facility—a child-development center 250 miles away—had an unexpected vacancy. The director considered the applications of several children, with Darrell at the top of the list. If I was interested in placing Darrell, I had to call her right away. I wrote down her number.

"Karen." I sobbed as my friend answered the phone. She instantly recognized the pain in my voice. She talked to me soothingly until I calmed down. I gasped out the urgency of my call. My dear friend would support me in whatever decision I made. She talked to my heart and then to my head. She reminded me that I could go "check out" the center before I agreed to let Darrell stay. She urged me to take a walk and to pray. Then I was to call the director for specifics.

With a warm, grandmotherly voice, the center's director answered, but with the knowledge of a general, she spoke of her program. What she said impressed me. Then I was shocked to learn that Darrell would have to be at the center—a six-hour drive—on Saturday, only four days away. I in no way was prepared to abandon my son, with only a few days notice, to strangers in a foreign place. Could I take the chance of waiting months or years for another opening? Stammering, my eyes filled with tears, I answered, "Yes." We would be there.

Before Saturday Darrell needed to have a physical exam, a health certificate, shot records, prescription refills, specific clothing, and personal-hygiene articles. Personnel there assured me that I could leave him for a few days' trial or could refuse to admit him if I believed that the facility was not in his best interest.

I hung up the phone, closed my door, and cried. And prayed.

Darrell definitely would benefit from consistent, 24-hour training and care in a structured, therapeutic environment. A rotating staff would make sure he was safe. His exhausted mother and large family were not functioning well with the constant turmoil and stress that Darrell's behavior caused. I had to admit that he had become unmanageable. As much as we all loved him, our conglomerate family had so many other problems that we were not helping him to grow. Dealing with him prevented individual kids, with their own issues, from getting the attention they needed.

My closed door had attracted my other kids. They heard my crying and called out, "Mom, what's wrong?" They knocked on the door.

I got off my knees, grabbed tissues for my nose and eyes, and opened the door. The kids—all subdued—filed in and sat down. They listened while I struggled, through tears, to explain what had happened so suddenly. I told them the decisions I had to make. They were as upset as I was and were confused with the urgency. Each kid objected. Each said I was wrong to send him away now. I should wait a year or so. I could see that my decision threatened their own security. Each one thought, "What if I'm next?"

Three of my teens already had experienced short stays in residential psychiatric facilities. They had gone to these facilities for post-traumatic stress disorders, oppositional-defiance disorders, and other emotional problems because of abuse and abandonment. I took all the blame for this decision as the best option for Darrell. I couldn't add to their personal trauma by letting them know that the stress of dealing with Darrell, seven young teens, and a baby was getting to be more than I could deal with. I had made a commitment to these children, too.

After much discussion the kids agreed that we would take Darrell just to check out the place. The next three days flashed by with doctors' visits, packing, and a tearful trip to Darrell's school to say good-bye to his teachers and therapists. On Friday Darrell returned from school on the bus. Tina was with him. The school had given him a good-bye party. He wore a t-shirt that the teachers and the children in his class signed with painted handprints. Tina handed me a large, handmade card that read, "We will miss you, Darrell."

I cried again. Sniffling back tears, I told Tina that we weren't sure about this yet. Maybe the party was premature. I trusted in God's timing for the inevitable, but I prayed that it wasn't too soon. Maybe He was making this easier on me by keeping us busy so that I couldn't grieve yet. Besides, if I didn"t like the facility, I could change my mind about the placement.

Saturday at 6 a.m., we drove along the same highway that I had traveled to bring Darrell into my family six years before. The hectic pace of the previous week had left me numb. Usually, driving was my thinking and praying time, but with nine rambunctious kids in the van, I was aware of my inability to concentrate. I only could pray over and over, "Oh, God, let me do the right thing."

I became mesmerized by the passing trees. I almost was oblivious to the roar of childish antics. When squealing turned into squalling, we made pit stops for the bathroom and snacks.

Cruising over the crest of a hill, we arrived at a long, low building that was built like a Fifties motel. A small group of boys, some in wheelchairs, loitered near the building's covered entrance. A casually dressed young woman rose from a bench to greet us. Since we had arrived at lunchtime, I had planned to let the director know that we were in town and that we would go eat a picnic lunch. We'd bring Darrell back later.

The kids waited, playing with Darrell, in a small waiting room while I was escorted to the nurses' station and then into the director's office. The friendly staff was expecting us. The staff members wanted to meet Darrell immediately.

The director, a middle-aged matron with a professional manner and a warm smile, greeted us. A tall, quiet man who was in charge of the unit to which Darrell would be assigned greeted all my kids and me with honest interest and humor. The staff members treated Darrell as if they already knew him. The tall man took Darrell's hand. He invited all the kids to go on a tour with him.

The director was my tour guide. She readily answered my many questions. The building was depressingly bare but functional in design. The staff's friendliness and obvious attempts to decorate the residents' rooms made the place look less institutional.

The children aimlessly played or wandered around within sight of a staff person. They all appeared happy and clean. The director and I concluded our tour at her office and began a mutual interview.

Near the dining room Darrell and my other kids met up with us. He received a seat and a lunch tray, so staff members could observe his self-help skills. With food he was happy. Self-feeding was one of Darrell's few accomplishments, once he had figured out that I would not feed him. He had developed a good appetite and could spoon- or finger-feed himself.

I surveyed the cafeteria. One-on-one, the staff helped children with their meals. Many of the kids were in wheelchairs. Two ambulatory teen-agers, staring into space, appeared to be autistic. A large, retarded boy danced over to me and grabbed at my car keys. I joked with him as I told him he couldn't have the keys. A worker spoke to him respectfully. The worker used a cracker to distract him and steered him back to his seat.

A little girl crept on a floor mat near a low window. With extreme effort she pulled herself up to stand in the sunlight. She shook her head and laughed to herself. She, too, was blind. Many of these kids functioned as infants. Here, Darrell's development would be "average." He had the advantage of being able to walk. Many of the others were not mobile. I recognized the necessity for structure and for the uncluttered environment for their safety. The facility impressed me favorably.

I confided to the sympathetic director my reservations about leaving Darrell. After much discussion we agreed that Darrell should stay for a two-week trial. Hesitantly my older kids agreed with me. Not too willingly, they brought his clothes in from the van. The kids went outside to play catch in the parking lot. I hugged Darrell. Off he went to the day room with the staff, while I returned to the director's sunny office to fill out papers. The director looked up and said that I could go. Go? I had not said "good-bye." We had not had our picnic. How could I just leave?

Tears clouded my eyes. I started to shake her hand; then I accepted and returned her hug. My emotions in turmoil, I turned, left her office, and somehow walked out of the building. I could not allow my grief to upset Darrell. I could hear him happily playing in the distant room.

My kids asked where Darrell was. I couldn't speak. I got in the driver's seat and gripped the steering wheel. My children piled into the van in awkward silence and then exploded, "Where's Darrell?"

"He's staying," I stammered. They argued with me. They objected to leaving him without saying "good-bye." I lowered my head on my arms, with my hand clenched on the wheel, and choked back sobs. I cried. We cried together. My kids were understandably angry. They accused the place of kidnapping him and me of deserting him.

"Oh, God. What have I done? Give me the right words. Give me a peace to know that I've done the right thing for all my children," I prayed anxiously. I felt many pairs of eyes drilling into the back of my head.

I wiped my eyes, blew my nose, and took a deep breath. I turned to face my accusers. Carefully choosing my words, I tried to explain that the center was a good, safe place for Darrell. We all knew that he didn't understand "good-bye." Leaving him when he was happy was better, easier.

They reluctantly agreed that we didn't want to leave him having a tantrum. I assured them that we would be back in a couple of weeks to make sure he was okay. We could take him home if any problems arose. My kids got unusually quiet.

Nick whispered, "What if he isn't happy?"

Cora added, "What if they hurt him?"

"When is he coming home?"

"What about our picnic with him?"

Separation anxiety. Desertion. Abuse. Old memories and old fears surfaced. On the long trip home we explored answers to many questions, especially those unasked.

"He is still my son. He always will be your brother."

As the miles separated us, my kids began to be more positive. Now we could go to McDonalds and to the movies. We could attend school activities, church, and Scouts even if we couldn't find a babysitter for Darrell. These kids who had been through so much themselves could not allow more pain into their lives. They were survivors. They searched for the positive and buried the pain.

* * * * *

With school beginning, the next few weeks were hectic. Calls to the facility director reassured me that Darrell was fine. We delayed our return visit. My teaching assignment was tiring. Keeping house, caring for the kids, and juggling their activities was exhausting, but I felt guilty that I did not have to worry about Darrell. As much as the kids and I wanted to see him, we all were reluctant to face the 12-hour trip.

I reserved a campground cabin that was near Darrell's school. We could swim in the campground pool and have a cookout with Darrell. By using a cabin and our camper, I'd feel safer having Darrell spend the night with us.

Our long, tiring trip behind us, I left the gang playing outside Darrell's "home" while I went in to get him. Before I saw him dancing down the hall with the staff, I heard him giggling. The supervisor said, "Darrell, someone is here to see you."

"Hi?" he said.

"Hi, Darrell!" I blubbered. I hugged him tight as he tackled my waist. As I tried to regain my composure, I talked nonsense to him.

"Mama?" he questioned.

"Yes, Darrell, Mama is here." I stammered, as tears ran own my face.

I was shocked that he recognized my voice. He looked so much bigger. His top permanent teeth were growing in. He needed a haircut; his hair always was a struggle. Always excited about going outdoors, he pulled me toward the exit. His brothers and sisters welcomed him with hugs and put him in the van. I gathered up extra clothing and diapers so we could take him to the campground for the afternoon.

While I fixed sandwiches for a picnic lunch, the kids played with Darrell on the playground and went for walks. He devoured a sandwich and demanded more chips. We all changed into swimsuits. Off to the fenced-in pool we trekked.

Much too soon a chilly breeze forced us out of the pool. I had the usual struggle getting Darrell out of the water, dried off, and changed. I finally could relax a little while my other kids, with Darrell in hand, explored the campground.

I had a short conference with the director before I left the center and was satisfied that he was being well-treated. The center was monitoring his medication, dealing with his tantrums, and making schooling and therapy plans that were consistent with his needs. We also had agreed that returning to the center for the night would be best for Darrell. We didn't want to break his routine.

Considerate of the kids' objections, I explained the change of plans. I timed Darrell's return to the center so that he would arrive just in time for supper. Hopefully the smell of food and a return to his schedule would make leaving him easier. Not wanting to go inside, he balked at the entrance, but a wise staff member had a dinner plate in her hand and coaxed him into the dining room.

As we returned to the campground, the kids questioned again the purpose of returning him early and not letting him spend the night. They commented that he hadn't wanted to go inside. Maybe he didn't like the center. I helped them to remember that he had always preferred to be outside and not in.

Cora echoed my thoughts that Darrell needed a haircut. We all laughed as we recalled what an endeavor that was. Someone mentioned seeing a bruise on his arm where the center had drawn his blood. We had seen another bruise on his head, where the center told me that he hit his head during a tantrum. Nick was concerned that people at the center were hurting him. I tried to reassure my kids, and myself, that Darrell always had bruised easily from falls and tantrums.

The pain of parting was not as intense as the first time. We returned to the campground for a cookout—a special outing for the rest of the family. That night, as they played on the playground by the light of the moon, I sat on a much-too-small swing and gazed at the stars. The full moon was hidden by alternate bands of high cirrus clouds. It allowed the stars to shine brightly.

I watched my beautiful children chasing each other in the moonlight. I wondered about their futures and Darrell's future. I recalled telling my oldest daughters that my job as their parent was to teach them to be good citizens, responsible adults, and most importantly, Christians.

These kids had faced traumas that would affect their lives, but I knew that God was in control. They would survive and fulfill God's purpose for their lives. I was proud and happy to be a part of that plan. What about Darrell? What could possibly be God's plan for him? He would never become a responsible adult or a good citizen. He couldn't make a decision to accept Christ.

What purpose did the stars have? The moon gave light to enable the kids to play, but when clouds covered the moon, the light of the beautiful stars was insignificant. We love stars for what they are. Perhaps this was like Darrell. God values him and loves him just because He made him. Darrell doesn't have to prove anything to anyone. He is God's creation.

* * * * *

In October I attended a teacher's conference. I was alone and without the kids. The conference was about an hour's drive from Darrell's center, so I planned for a short, unannounced visit. Darrell was the same. Again he greeted me with, "Mama?"

I took him to a park, where he played on the ground while I sat in a swing, observing.

"He will probably spend his life in institutions," I mumbled to myself, as I shook my head sadly. In six years he had not progressed six months developmentally. I watched him swish his hand through the sand at the base of the slide. He stared at me with blank eyes but responded when I called his name. I lifted him onto my lap. We swung higher and higher. He laughed loudly and shook his head from side to side. The breeze blew his long hair in golden swirls across his sightless, blue eyes.

Returning to the center at lunchtime, Darrell refused to enter. I gave him one end of a curly telephone cord. He shook it and made it vibrate but refused to let me lead him by the cord into the building. Trying to convince him to go inside sent him into a kicking, screaming tantrum. He loved the outdoors and did not like to be confined, but I had to go back to the conference.

The director heard the commotion. She calmly walked outside, kicked off her shoes, and, talking gently, grabbed Darrell in a bear hug from behind. He directed a kick at her legs. I grabbed his feet. We lifted him off the ground, thrashing and screaming, and carried him into the center.

Safely inside, we lowered him onto the carpet, where he repeatedly banged his head until she talked him "down." I quietly backed away to observe and left him to their care. A kitchen staff member hurried down the hall. She gave him a sandwich on a paper plate. Darrell reached for it an then followed her quietly to the lunchroom.

With a finger over her lips to indicate that we should be quiet, the director motioned me toward her office.She explained that Darrell usually was compliant unless a change of routine occurred or unless he had to go inside from their playground. Darrell attended special classes at a public school. This meant he could ride his beloved school bus. If the bus was late in the morning, he became impatient. After school a snack waited to encourage him to leave the bus and go inside. We agreed that he could not think of the future, so he did not associate his having just gone inside with the fact that I was leaving.

* * * * *

A notice from the Social Security office set my nerves on edge. The office had arranged a hearing to review Darrell's case. I thought all of this had been settled long ago. Social Security still demanded $4,000 I didn't have. I knew that I had followed the law. Every year I had updated his case. I knew I could justify his needs. I pulled out all of his old records, organized doctors' reports, and made pages of notes. I wrote letters and gathered supporting evidence of Darrell's eligibility. Fortunately I had saved everything, even if stuff wasn't in good order. I had old correspondence with Social Security. That correspondence included their psychologist's report. To my file I added a recent photograph of Darrell.

On the morning of the scheduled appointment, I took off from work. My palms were sweaty and my blouse wet with nervous perspiration. Officials ushered me into a small, sterile room furnished with a long, lone table and three chairs. A large, solemn, middle-aged man in the intimidating robes of a judge sat at the far end of the table, opposite the door. He pushed up his wire-framed glasses and looked bored as he thumbed through a file of papers. Officials led me to the opposite end of the lengthy table, near the door. A court-reporter's machine was situated on the table about halfway between us. Three or four microphones marched down the center of the table between the judge and me.

An eternity of silence was dispelled slightly when a mousy, older woman carrying a legal pad crept into the room to seat herself by the machine. Her hand poised over the record button.

Clearing his throat, the judge looked up. He introduced himself. He tried to ease my anxiety by stating that he did not work for Social Security but was impartial. The reporter began to transcribe.

The judge's questions were easier to answer than I had expected. I had plenty of documents. Using my notes, I told him about Darrell's birth history and adoption; the CPS transfer of benefits to me as payee; my many, long visits to the local Social Security office; the names of the people who had interviewed me; and the psychiatrist's evaluation.

After another 30 minutes of questioning, I pulled Darrell's photo out of my file and caught my breath. I intended to show it to the judge so he could see for himself the face of a blind, retarded child. Before I could pass him the photo, the judge decided in my favor. He had the mikes cut off. I broke into tears as I tried to thank him.

"Don't you understand, lady?" the judge asked. "I said you don't have to pay back the money."

I nodded, "Yes." I handed him the photo of Darrell while I tried to get my emotions under control.

"Sir, I do understand, and I thank you. But I have to tell you that Darrell no longer is able to live at home. He's in an institution now because I can't deal with him," I said painfully.

"The center's director said that they would seek his SSI to fund his tuition. How can they do that since the SSI was cut off?" I knew that without this funding, I could not afford the cost of his placement, nor could I bring him home.

The judge answered that the center might take custody of Darrell. I never intended to lose custody! I was shocked. I could not talk at all.

I gathered up my papers, whispered a "thank you" to the judge, and left. How could I balance the relief of not owing all that money with the possibility of losing my son?

My heart was in such turmoil that I had to talk to someone I trusted. Praying, I drove directly to the adoption agency. I cried out to my friend, our family's worker. She was supportive of my feelings. She never had heard of a facility taking custody of a child to obtain SSI, but then, Darrell was the first adopted child she had placed that had to be placed in a long-term residential facility.

Returning home, I called Karen and asked her to visit me. We closed the door to my study. I stumbled over the events of the day and told her what happened with the judge and with the social worker. I realized that I had not resolved my feelings of loss and guilt. The threat of losing custody of this child, for whom I could no longer care, brought me face to face with pain caused by believing I had failed him.

With Karen's encouragement, I took slow, deep breaths. I tried to relate the facts to my feelings of frustration. Karen lis-

115

tened attentively to my rambling. I felt fragile but strangely more secure. Finally the weight began to release.

We became aware that some of my kids were crowded around the closed door. Voices asked, "What's wrong, Mom?"

Karen answered them that nothing that involved them was wrong. The door rattled. We heard them whispering. My best friend and I shook our heads and smiled. She gave me a much-needed hug. She pulled the door open and broke the tension for us all.

We invited the kids into the room. I tried to help them understand all that had happened that day that had caused me so much pain. I couldn't tell if they really understood why I was upset, but they seemed satisfied. I prayed that each one would realize that admitting feelings and fears was healthy and normal. How relieved I was to have worked through this trial and to begin to let go!

* * * * *

Darrell turned 10 years old. We all went to visit. He was the same. Holding a staff person's hand, he danced down the hall.

"Mama? Mamamama?" he greeted me. He seemed very happy to see us.

I rushed up to him and hugged him tight. No longer did I squat down, for his head was up to my shoulder. He hugged me around the waist, pulled away, grabbed my hand, and danced toward the nurse's station. In the lobby the other kids caught him up in hugs.

Rain poured. We could not go to a playground today. I took all the kids to the YMCA, where the older kids played pool and ping-pong. Chris, now two years old, and Darrell grabbed the balls and got in the other kids' way. Chris' actions were deliberate. Darrell's behavior was erratic. Both kids became tired and frustrated. I could reason with Chris and distract him with another activity. Darrell had a tantrum and had to be carried from the room. The rain stopped, so we went outside into an enclosed patio. Darrell wandered aimlessly. Chris purposefully explored. Darrell interacted infrequently, ignored us, and threw another tantrum. Both boys needed their diapers changed.

TWELVE

God's Purpose

"Before I formed you in the womb I knew you, before you were born I set you apart . . ." (Jer. 1:5).

Baby Chris, now 12, accompanied me to visit Darrell when Darrell turned 20. No longer do we travel six hours each way for our visits. At 16 Darrell was transferred to a larger, adult facility that was one-and-a-half hours away. This facility closed a few years later. Then, an organization in Houston accepted him. This organization provided for small groups of adult clients in suburban homes in ordinary neighborhoods.

The hour's drive took us down a residential street in a middle-class neighborhood of brick homes with well-kept yards. I prompted Chris to locate the house where he thought Darrell might live. A man mowed his own lawn, while kids rode bikes on the quiet street. Nothing distinguished Darrell's residence from the other homes.

Chris waited in the van. A young Jamaican lady answered my knock at the front door. She said that Darrell was ready for our outing. He heard my voice and said, "Mama?"

"Yes, Darrell. Mama is here." I gave and received a bear hug.

"Car?" he demanded, pulling on my hand.

I checked with the caretaker to make sure Darrell had on an adult diaper and told her the approximate time we would return.

Impatient to be off, Darrell jerked the doorknob.

"Okay, Darrell, we're going. First I have to unlock the door."

Darrell grunted as he bounced up and down. He tugged at the partially opened door and slammed it back against the wall. Pulling me along the sidewalk, he asked, "Car?"

"Yes, we're going for a ride in the car," I assured him.

Opening the van's passenger door. I helped him climb into the bucket seat. I fastened his seat belt. Chris said "Hi" to Darrell and handed him a children's paperback book.

Darrell happily patted the book and then rapidly rubbed both of his hands over the cover. He carefully laid it on the floor and then picked up the magazine and rolled it up. Giggling, he patted the side of his face with the paper cylinder.

We drove to a neighborhood park that had a large, fenced playground and a few, covered picnic tables. I led Darrell through a gate onto the pebble-covered play area. Chris brought a small cooler and our picnic lunch. Darrell plopped down, frog-legged, on the gravel. He carefully placed his magazine by his side before he swished both hands rapidly over the pebbles. He giggled in delight.

Chris carried the picnic to one of the tables before he ran off to play. I sat on the pebbles beside Darrell. I carried on a one-sided conversation with him as he scooped up handfuls of pebbles. In a slow stream he released the gravel from hand to hand. I dropped pebbles onto his pants. He giggled and swished more pebbles onto his pants. For what seemed an eternity we played this game. I became bored long before he grew tired of the rocks.

Darrell got up and danced in place. I coaxed him over to the wooden playground so I could encourage him to climb up to the top of the small slide. He lifted his foot when I said, "Step up, Darrell."

When he was younger, Darrell liked to climb and slide. He would follow my directions to "step up, step down", and shuffled his feet if he wasn't sure of his footing. But today, the playground equipment didn't interest him.

He called, "Mama? Boo?"

Finding his magazine for him, I thought, "OK. Now what shall we do?"

Aimlessly he pulled me by the hand toward the far side of the playground. I led him to the swings. He turned, placed the magazine on the ground, and sat on the swing seat. I pushed him for a while. Giggling he pumped himself higher and higher. I squeezed into the next swing to join the fun.

I tired of the swings long before he did, probably because I didn't fit too comfortably. I slowed to a stop so I could watch the other children. Most of the kids ignored Darrell or stopped their play briefly to stare at him. No one walked over to swing with us. No mothers walked close enough for me to talk to them. I was accustomed to Darrell and me being the object of curiosity. I often wished I could gently enlighten the onlookers.

Darrell began dragging his feet back and forth to make furrows in the pebbles. Suddenly he plopped down on the ground to play in the rocks. Fortunately the swing seat was rubber, so when it hit him in the back of the head, it was only annoying, not hurtful. He swatted at it. He leaned way over and became prone on the stones.

Darrell tired again of the pebbles, stood up, and stood before me. He raised his hand to his mouth and asked, "Eee?"

"Sure, we'll go eat." As I called Chris, we made our way back to the table. Darrell put his magazine on the table. I wiped his hands. In anticipation he sat on a bench. I unwrapped a sandwich, put it on a paper plate, and placed his hand on it.

Chris added chips to Darrell's plate. Darrell squirmed, shook himself with pleasure, and giggled. He used both hands to cram the sandwich half into his mouth. He felt the plate to locate the chips and passed over the rest of the sandwich.

Putting down the last bite of crust, he said "k,k", meaning drink, or more specifically, a cola. I placed a canned drink in his hand. He gulped down most of it and then felt the table for a spot by his plate to set it down. He continued eating chips.

While on the playground, Darrell had attracted the attention of several children who had kept an eye on him while they continued their play. Two young girls, running from the slides to a table where their mother was setting out lunch, stopped near our table to gawk at Darrell's bad manners.

"Hi", I said to the girls. "He can't see. He's blind."

"Hi?" repeated Darrell.

"He can't talk much, either."

"Girls, come over here and eat lunch. Don't bother them," called their mom.

"They're okay," I interjected. "They're just curious."

Satisfied for now, the two girls ran to their table.

Pushing back his empty plate. Darrell got off the bench. He danced back over to the pebbles and plopped down, frog-legged, to again swish his hands back and forth across their surface. He gathered up a handful of rocks and then let them stream from hand to hand. He rubbed handfuls onto his thighs.

I stayed at the table to clean up while Chris ran off to play. Darrell had left his magazine on the table, but I was sure he had not forgotten it.

As I sat at the table, I relaxed and watched him. Darrell relished in the simplicity—food and drink, doing whatever he chose, the texture of pebbles, the feel of the breeze. His giggles expressed his simple joy in life.

Darrell got up. He shuffled his feet in the rocks as he walked back toward me.

"Tee, tee," he said, as he crossed his fingers in universal sign language to indicate restroom.

"OK, Darrell," I sighed. The dreaded moment. The park had no restrooms. Calling Chris to help, I gathered up our cooler and picnic lunch. We hurried to the van.

The closest public restroom was at a service station several miles away. I led Darrell through the store to the restrooms at the rear. I took him into the unoccupied ladies room and locked the door.

"Tee, tee," Darrell reminded me.

His diaper was soaked. I had forgotten to bring a replacement.

"Well, son, I see that we're going to go back to the house for a change."

I removed the soaking diaper from my man-son and prayed that we'd get back to the house with a dry van.

Darrell seemed to know that we were back at the house. He grunted, grumbled, and threw himself back and forth as I tried to unbuckle his seat belt. I gave him his book and magazine in hopes he would settle down.

Chris handed him a plastic spring toy. I grabbed the other end and shook it to coax him out of the van. He shook the spring and pulled on it as I led him up the sidewalk to the house. Reaching the door, he shook the spring violently and then shook himself in anger. The caretaker answered my knock. She opened the door for me to lead a reluctant young man into the living room. He suddenly turned toward the door and ran into Chris, who followed with a birthday cake. Realizing that the door was closed and locked, Darrell hit with both hands, lashed out at it with hard kicks, and butted his head on the door. He screamed. The diaper would have to wait.

"It's okay, Darrell. Come over here. We're going to have some cake."

He ignored me, threw himself frog-legged on the floor, and kicked at the door. He screamed. He hit the door with his book. Neither the caretaker nor I dared to get close enough to intercede. She said not to worry and that he would calm down soon. She went to get his tape player.

She returned with loud music playing and encouraged Darrell to take the player. Still screaming and kicking, he threw down the book, grabbed the tape player, and jammed it to his ear.

I invited Darrell's housemates to the table to have birthday cake. A girl in her mid-20s grunted a reply and zigzagged her wheelchair toward the kitchen. The other resident stared blankly at me, flapped her hands, squealed, and danced toward the table.

Calmed by his music, Darrell got up off the floor. Still grumbling, he arrived at the table. Chris had backed off to sit on a couch away from the action. He refused to join the party. The caretaker settled Darrell and the others around the table. She cut and served everyone a piece of cake.

I caught her eye and mouthed that we were going to leave. I always hated sneaking away without saying "good-bye", but we both knew that the sound of my voice would counter his attention to the music and cake and would set off another tantrum.

Tiptoeing to the door, I carefully opened it. Chris and I departed. Would Darrell tantrum when he realized we were gone? Would he even know we'd been there? What does he know?

* * * * *

On the long drive home, Chris fell asleep. I fell into my habit of prayer-driving. I asked the Lord to help me understand His purpose for Darrell's life. I still was having trouble accepting Darrell as God did.

Darrell will never be "educated" beyond the two-year-old level. His IQ, based on his functioning ability and his age, had been determined to be 13. He always will be totally dependent on others for his personal needs and daily care. His seizures are under medical control, but medication has not eliminated frequent, violent tantrums.

How does God view Darrell? For almost 20 years I have agonized over this. I try to remind myself of the beautiful stars that don't have the brightness of the full moon but have purpose for guidance—for giving direction. I know God is compassionate and loving. He allowed, not caused, Darrell's injuries. Only He knows how Darrell will guide the lives of others.

I think back over the lives of the special students that I have had the privilege of teaching. Shawn recently attained the rank of Eagle Scout. I wept with others as he stumbled, even with his canes, up the few steps to receive his award—the highest achievement in Scouting. He now is an architecture student at a local college. I remember Zack as a preschooler zipping on his skateboard to class. The skateboard compensated for his legs. He was born with only stumps. Last year Zack played football with the junior-high team. He ran on his muscular hands and arms and dragged his useless stumps. I recall so many other "stars" that don't shine as brightly but whom a loving God also created.

Would I have adopted Darrell when he was age three if I had known that, 17 years into the future, he would not be a senior in high school but would be functioning as he did at age three? I would say "yes." If I had known about all the other children that would become part of my family, at that time, I believe I might have said "no." Looking back, I see that if Darrell had not been in our family my other children would have been denied positive guidance.

I am disappointed and heartbroken that I could not make a great difference in Darrell's life. Most people have commented how they wished a cute kitten or puppy or baby could stay little, but tragedy occurs when a person remains mentally an infant.

What impact has Darrell's life had on my family and me? My 11 other children and the numerous foster children who have lived with Darrell have learned compassion and not to be judgmental. One of my foster daughters gave birth to a severely handicapped child. She is caring for him with love, joy, and acceptance.

Recently my adopted daughter introduced her three children to Darrell as her brother. She was able to explain his peculiarities. After a brief period of curiosity they accepted his differences and ran off to play. Nick and Chris relate especially well to Darrell. They are sensitive to him and anticipate his needs.

I wondered: Did adoption make a difference in Darrell's life? Since he can't communicate, we'll never know his thoughts. I hope that by being in a loving, although, at times, chaotic, family, Darrell experienced the love and security to develop to his greatest potential.

The devastation of child abuse is that no one can predict the outcome physically, mentally, or emotionally for the child. All children need loving, caring families who are willing to do their best for the child. Special-needs children require special families. That specialness is simply a family's willingness to step out in faith.

DARRELL'S FAMILY ALBUM

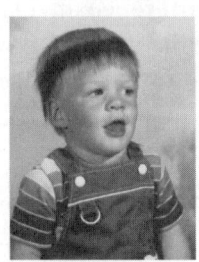

18 Months

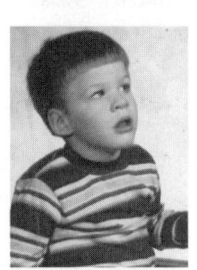

2 Years

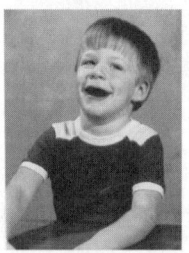

3 Years

At age 6

At age 10

Uncooperative kids at photo session, 1989:
Carol, Darrell, Cora, Christina in front row;
Nick, Grace, Roy, Phillip in middle row;
Colleen, Joe, JoAnna in back row

The family in 1987:
Cora, Darrell, Carol in front; Nick,
Grace, JoAnna in back.

How to order more copies of *Adopting Darrell*

and Carol Weishampel's first book, *Grandma's on the Go*
CALL: 1-800-747-0738
FAX: 1-888-252-3022
Email: orders@hannibalbooks.com
Write: Hannibal Books
P.O. Box 461592
Garland, Texas 75046
Visit: *www.hannibalbooks.com*

Number of copies of *Adopting Darrell* _____
Number of copies of *Grandma's on the Go* _____
Multiply total number of copies: _____ by $9.95 =
Total cost of books: $_____

Add $3 for postage and handling for first book and add 50-cents for each additional book in the order.
Shipping total $_____
Texas residents add 8.25 % sales tax $_____

Total order $_____
number on check enclosed _____
credit card # _____ exp. date_____
(Visa, MasterCard, Discover, American Express accepted)

Name _____

Address _____

City State, Zip _____

Phone _____

Email _____